i·ching readings
INTERPRETING THE ANSWERS

i·ching readings

Interpreting the Answers

NEW REVISED EDITION

INTERPRETED BY WU WEI

POWER PRESS
LOS ANGELES, CALIFORNIA

Library of Congress Control Number: 2005926777

ISBN: 0-943015-43-X

New Revised Edition 10 9 8 7 6 5 4 3 2 1

For information, address:

> Power Press
> 6428 Meadows Court
> Malibu, California, 90265
> Telephone: 310/392-9393
> E-mail: wuwei@power-press.com
> Website: www.power-press.com

Cover design: Roger Gefvert
Interior design and production: Robert S. Tinnon Design
All interior art by Wu Wei

The symbol on the title page is the Chinese word picture for change.
It was painted with five quick slashes of Wu Wei's ink brush.

This book is dedicated to Fu Hsi, who deserves all credit for the creation of the I Ching, to King Wen, who renamed all the kua during his year in prison in 1143 B.C., and to his son Tan, known as the Duke of Chou, who added the meaning and text to all 384 lines, completed in 1109 B.C.

This book is also dedicated to all those seekers of wisdom who came after them and who have kept the wisdom alive and intact for thousands of years—and to those of you who will partake of this great wisdom and carry it forward through the ages.

FU HSI RISING FROM THE MOUNTAIN
DESIGNING THE EIGHT GREAT SIGNS.

Contents

PART THREE:
A BRIEF HISTORY
OF THE I CHING 229

AUTHOR'S APOLOGY TO
WOMEN READERS

I sincerely apologize for using he, his, him when speaking generally. Using he/she throughout becomes cumbersome for the reader and disturbs the flow of thought. I chose to use the masculine form because it is what we are accustomed to seeing in print and because the goal is to make the reading easy.

AUTHOR'S APOLOGY TO ALL READERS

I humbly apologize to you for my presumption that I know something that you do not and for my egotistical assumption that I know anything at all. All information comes from one source, the Universe, and since we are all part of it, its information belongs to us all and is available to each of us. On the small chance that I have spent more time seeking out information about the I Ching and ways to use it than you have, and therefore may have received information which you may not have yet received, and because I want you to have as much information as possible about the I Ching, I risk this great presumption. Please overlook and forgive my immodesty. That I undertake this work at all is only because of my love for the great wisdom and my sincere desire to impart it to you.

Your humble and insignificant servant,

AUTHOR'S NOTES

In this book, the word *Universe* is capitalized to acknowledge its greatness, its uniqueness, its complete originality, but other words used to refer to the Universe, such as *it*, are not capitalized because that practice seems to detract from the flow of thought.

English speaking people call the six-line figures *hexagrams*. The Chinese call them *kua*. In this book, as in my other books, I refer to them as kua, (pronounced "gwa," with the "a" sounded as in father), which means symbol.

In the section titled "Readings," I have given examples of questions asked and answers received. After each question I write the text of both the kua and the moving lines so you can read the answers on the same page without going to another source or location. I do that, even in the case where a kua has been earlier written.

Acknowledgments

I want to thank Roger Gefvert for his enlightened cover design, which set the standard for the beauty of the book and reflects so well the look and feel of the timeless quality of the I Ching itself.

And I want to thank Robert Tinnon for his inspired interior design and layout, which correspond so well to the cover and to the clarity and spirituality of the I Ching.

Introduction

If you knew which of your actions would bring you good fortune and which misfortune, which actions would lead to your success and which to failure, would that knowledge not be better than gold and diamonds? Would it not allow you to achieve any goal? Have anything you desired? If you could transcend the barriers of time to look into the future, into the past, if you could see the road that led to happiness, the road to despair, would you not consider yourself fortunate indeed?

When you become adept in the use of the I Ching, you will be able to do all those things and more. Open your mind to the words on the following pages; allow yourself the freedom, the luxury, to believe that all of the above is possible.

We are part of the Universe—each one of us—as much a part as are the galaxies that whirl through space and, here on our little planet, as much a part as are the trees, the mountains, and the sky. We are no less a part of the Universe than anything else is or was or ever can be. We are an integral part, made of the same stuff as the rest of the Universe: Universal energy. All *is* one.

The Universe is alive, conscious, and aware—acutely aware of each of us. And how could it be otherwise since we are it? The Universe experiences itself through us . . . and through the breeze blowing through the trees, the snail crawling on the ground, the lightning that strikes the mountain top, and the galaxies that whirl through space.

The Universe wants to continue. How do we know? Because it does . . . that means that all the laws of the Universe are in favor of continuation. If there was even one law that favored discontinuation, surely destruction would have come to pass during the billions of years since it all began. But, it has not come to pass. That also means that everything that happens is perfect—must be perfect—that the Universe will not tolerate anything less. If it could, it would be in danger of its own destruction because one imperfect event could lead to two, to three, to four, and so on, leading to destruction. It never allows even the first imperfect event to occur. That means that since we are the Universe, a part of it, everything that happens benefits us. It may hurt us or take something away from us, but it always benefits us. If we act on the basis of that, Universal law will bring peace to our souls and joy to our hearts.

Everything that happens, happens within time. We like to think that time stretches illimitably forward into the future and illimitably back into the past while we exist on a hairline of time that separates the future from the past, the hairline we call *Now*. Quite the reverse is true; all there is and was and ever will be is an endless "Now," within which change occurs.

Within that endless "Now," we are eternal, all of us, as is everything else, simply changing—endlessly.

Because we are the Universe, a part of it, and because time is a living, breathing entity that contains consciousness—may indeed *be* the consciousness of the Universe, permeating everything, including ourselves—we can know everything the Universe knows; all we need is a key to unlock that fount of sublime wisdom and complete information. That we each have a key is unquestionable; every time a new idea seems to arise spontaneously within us we have used our key. Egotistically, we like to think that we created the idea, but actually what we did was no less noteworthy: we channeled the idea from the source; we used our key. We know that the Universe wants us to have that knowledge because we have been provided with the key.

That the key exists within each of us is the premise of all divination. Divination surmises that there is a part of us that is at one with everything, including time, and therefore knows what everything knows. The English root word of divination is *divine*. The Latin root word is *divinus*, meaning a deity, and also, to foretell!

For us to be able to draw from the fount of Universal wisdom, we must have a means to do so. Some people draw from the fount with prayer; some by meditating; some by being quiet and focusing their attention on the subject under question, or no question at all; some by talking with psychics or astrologers; others by manipulating objects such as coins, tarot cards, ruins, yarrow stalks, or any of a number of related objects; still others by interpreting dreams.

All of the systems work perfectly, up to the limits of the systems and the capability of the questioner or interpreter. If, for instance, you ask a question and flip a coin to get an answer, you are limited to a yes or no answer. If you ask a question and select from a deck of cards with several sentences of guidance printed on it, you can obtain counsel beyond yes or no. The more sophisticated the system, the more complete and detailed will be the answer.

If you and I decided to formulate a system to obtain answers to questions, we would put into that system as many answers as there are questions. That may sound difficult, even impossible, but one answer can be sufficient for many questions. For instance, all questions regarding the taking of action can be generally satisfied with three answers: to take action, to take no action, or to delay taking action. Fortunately, we do not have to create a system of answers: the I Ching masterfully fills that need. Once the answers have been formulated, all that remains is to devise a method for determining which answer applies to which question. Because we are searching for cosmic answers, we must prevent ourselves from intellectually tampering with how we obtain the results, a method that will permit only the spiritual portion of ourselves—that portion that is at one with All-That-Is—to participate; the yarrow stalk method perfectly accomplishes that end.

When we close our eyes and grasp a number of yarrow stalks from a bunch of forty-nine stalks, when we select a card from a deck whose faces we cannot see, when we choose a stone from a pile of inscribed stones whose faces we cannot see, or in following similar practices, we exceed our intellectual ability to determine the outcome because we cannot know how many stalks were grasped, or which card was chosen until its face is seen, or which stone was chosen from the pile until the inscription on its face can be read. All such methods of choosing rely completely on the intuitive ability of the questioner, on his ability to draw upon his spiritual source that knows everything. In the words of Lao Tzu, ". . . to feel beyond touch . . . to hear beyond sound . . . to see beyond shape, and . . . to tell beyond words."

When all our answers have been developed and our method of selecting answers has been determined, we can proceed confidently to ask questions because there is a part within each of us that knows the answers to all our questions and that will guide us in choosing the correct answer.

Fu Hsi (pronounced *foo shee*), the great Chinese sage to whom the I Ching system is attributed, constructed his answers in the form of sixty-four six-line figures the Chinese call *kua*, each line stacked one above the other, either solid (—), or broken (- -). Each of the kua is formed by combining two of eight basic trigrams, which are three-line figures such as this: (≡ ≡). The two trigrams that form the kua (≣)are called *primary trigrams*. There are two other trigrams in the kua called *nuclear trigrams,* which will later be described in detail.

Before the lines exist, there are six empty spaces. The lines fill those spaces and move within them. Following the law of eternal change, the lines are always in motion, always moving upward. As a new line enters from the bottom, it pushes the five lines above it upward, thereby displacing the line at the top. The movement always follows the rhythm of the Universal heartbeat, always mirroring the Universe itself. Taken together, the kua and their lines represent every conceivable condition in Heaven and on Earth with all their states of change.

Each of the sixty-four kua can change into one another through the movement of one or more of the six lines that form the kua. There are 4,096 possible combinations (64 × 64), which represent every possible condition in Heaven and on Earth.

The kua and trigrams are both called *kua* (pronounced "gwa," with the "a" sounded as in father), which means *symbol*. To avoid confusion, but to retain the flavor of the ancient text as much as possible, the six-line figures will be referred to as *kua* and the three-line figures as *trigrams*.

Each of the sixty-four kua, with their combined total of 384 lines, represents a situation or condition. Each situation or condition contains the six stages of its own evolution:

1. about to come into being,
2. beginning,
3. expanding,
4. approaching maximum potential,
5. peaking, and
6. passing its peak and turning toward its opposite condition.

By taking the appropriate action, we can turn any condition into any other condition. (See my *A Tale of the I Ching*, Power Press)

The kua not only represent every conceivable situation and condition possible, but also include all their states of change. Fu Hsi's method for selecting the appropriate kua is unique: the manipulation of fifty yarrow stalks, one being laid aside as an observer stalk, the rest being divided and re-divided eighteen times.

Does the system work? Yes. Does it work perfectly? Yes. Every time? Yes. Will it work perfectly for you? Yes, if you seek the truth with reverence and sincerity. Why? Because you are a Divine Being in an eternal Universe of which you are an inseparable part, which is an inexhaustible wellspring of cosmic information from which you may freely draw. Can you draw from it correct answers to hurt another? No. Can you draw from it correct answers to gain an unfair advantage? No. Can you draw from it correct answers if you will misuse the information? No. All guidance given in the I Ching is virtuous, beneficial, and given with the intent of guiding you along the highest possible path for your greatest possible good and the greatest possible good of everyone and everything else. You will not be assisted by your higher self to commit acts harmful to yourself or to another.

Will frivolous questions be answered? Yes, frivolously. Will questions that imply doubt in the source of the answers be answered? Yes, but only in a way that will confirm the doubt in your mind; you cannot run a test on your own divinity.

How can you be certain the answers are correct? After you have received an answer to a vitally important question and feel everything within you resonating with the truth, wisdom, and guidance contained in the answer—a resonance so pure and sweet that it brings joy to your heart, and sometimes tears to your eyes—you will, at that moment, be certain that the question was perfectly answered, divinely answered. At those moments you can experience your oneness with All-That-Is. Once having had the experience, you will never again wonder who it is or what it is that is answering your questions or whether the answers are correct.

In the I Ching you can read that teaching is a holy task, to be withheld from no one. You can derive from that statement that the answers provided in the I Ching are given in the form of guidance, of teaching, which will not be withheld from you. Not only will you be provided with answers to questions, but you will also be given counsel concerning the best way to proceed to obtain a particular result. Additionally, under certain circumstances, you will be told what condition will replace the current condition. For the divine within you, time is not a barrier nor is distance.

Fu Hsi perceived the laws of the Universe and set them forth so that we could be guided, so that we could be free, so that we would no longer be subject to the tyranny of events, and so that each of us could be in charge of our own fate. He created the sixty-four kua so that we could know the operation of the Universe and so that within the Universe each of us could find our place. He spoke in terms of *good fortune* and *misfortune*. Good fortune brings you good friends, security, food, clothing, good health, shelter, opportunity, wealth, a good mate, and windfall good luck. Misfortune takes any or all of those same things away from you.

Fu Hsi spoke of the paths of life, calling the path that leads to good fortune "the way of the superior person" and the path that leads to misfortune "the way of the inferior person." The path of the superior person is the path of abundant life. That path is narrow in one sense and broad in another. It is narrow in that it does not stray into areas of dishonesty, selfishness, debauchery, harmful intentions, and unclean living. It is broad in the sense that it encompasses everything else that is in keeping with virtue, honor, clean living, good intentions, and integrity. The path of abundant life is filled with love, happiness, abundance, and success. We know when we are on that path when we are experiencing joy, happiness, and great good fortune. The path that leads away from abundant life can be discerned by our experiencing pain, unhappiness, and great misfortune. That path has many pitfalls, but they are of our own creation, even though it seems as if forces outside of us are creating them. The need for punishment arises when we have deviated from the path of abundant life and need the pitfalls to direct us back onto the correct path. Fu Hsi spoke in terms of *good* and *evil*. In modern times we rarely hear these terms used, but for this present work they have been preserved because they impart a sense of who Fu Hsi was, and they retain the flavor of the ancient texts.

We live in a perfect Universe in which only perfect events can unfold: the Universe will not tolerate anything else; if it could or would, it would be in danger of permitting its own destruction. That information must live in your consciousness if you are to lead a happy life, free of needless worry and frustration.

One of the great truths that can be gained from a study of the I Ching is that the Universe is powerfully inclined in our favor; there is more of the good force than the seeming bad force—that is why and how the Universe persists—and that is why you can always triumph over any evil force if you are good enough. The way to do that is not to combat evil directly—thereby becoming an instrument of evil—but to make energetic progress in the good, following Fu Hsi's path of the superior person that leads unerringly to the greatest states that humans can desire.

Remember that the greatest honor one can have is to be part of the Universe. You have been selected to have that honor. Remember also that the greatest spiritual experience one can have is simply to be who you are at any moment, including this one.

My fellow traveler, I wish you well. May you mount to the skies of success as though on the wings of six dragons!

Your humble and insignificant servant,

IT IS SAID OF THE ANCIENT BOOK OF WISDOM:

Neither far nor near,
neither dark nor deep
exist for it.

Wu Wei's comment:

Our questions are endless, but so are the answers: answers that provide perfect solutions for our most vital and difficult questions. That is because the Universe, the totally alive, completely aware Universe of which we are an inseparable part, wants us to have this profound knowledge that is so essential for our well-being. Nothing is hidden from it; it sees into the heart of everything.

part one

ABOUT THE

I CHING

As used in the title, *I* means *change*, and *Ching* means *book*; therefore, it is "The Book of Change," or, as it has come to be known, *The Book of Changes*. In my recently revised edition of the *I Ching*, I changed the subtitle to read *The Book of Answers*, as it more accurately describes the great book's function.

In the known Universe everything is constantly changing. For any book of wisdom or divination to portray the conditions of the Universe correctly—and to be useful—it must reflect the process of change. The I Ching masterfully reflects the ever-changing, ever-unfolding Universe.

Fu Hsi, the ancient Chinese sage who is known to us only in legend, is the man to whom we attribute the creation of the I Ching. He discovered the laws of the Universe and set them forth so that we could be guided, so that we could be free, so that we would no longer be subject to the tyranny of events, and so that each of us could be in charge of his or her own fate. He created the sixty-four kua so that we could know the operation of the Universe and so that within the Universe each of us could find our place. He spoke in terms of "good fortune" and "misfortune." Good fortune brings you good friends, security, food, clothing, good health, shelter, opportunity, wealth, a good mate, and windfall good luck. Misfortune takes any or all of those same things away from you.

Fu Hsi spoke of the paths of life, calling the path that leads to good fortune "the way of the superior person" and the path that leads to misfortune "the way of the inferior person." (At the back of this book are listed some of the qualities of the superior person.) He spoke in terms of "good" and "evil." In modern times we rarely hear those terms used, but for this present work they have been preserved because they impart a sense of who Fu Hsi was, and they retain the flavor of the ancient texts.

Everything that happens, happens within time. We like to think that time stretches illimitably forward into the future and illimitably back into the past while we exist on a tiny hairline of time that separates the future from the past, the hairline we call, "now." Quite the reverse is true; all there is and was and ever can be is an endless now, within which change occurs.

Within that endless now, we are eternal, as is everything else, all of us and everything simply going through endless change.

Because we are a part of the Universe, and because time is a living, breathing entity that contains consciousness—may indeed *be* the consciousness of the Universe, permeating everything, including ourselves—we can know everything the Universe knows; all we need is a key to unlock that fount of sublime wisdom and complete information. That we have a key is unquestionable; every time a new idea seems to arise spontaneously, we have used our key. Egotistically, we like to think that we created the idea, but actually what we did was no less noteworthy: we channeled the idea from the source; we used our key.

That the key exists within each of us is the premise of all divination. Divination surmises that there is a part of us that is at one with everything, including time, and therefore knows what everything knows. The English root word of divination is *divine*. The Latin root word is *divinus*, meaning a deity, and also, to foretell.

The *I Ching* is a book of answers. The answers are in the form of sixty-four situations or conditions that English speaking people call *hexagrams* and the Chinese call *kua*. Each situation or condition contains the six stages of its own evolution:

1. about to come into being,
2. beginning,
3. expanding,

4. approaching maximum potential,
5. peaking,
6. passing its peak and turning toward its opposite condition.

The sixty-four kua contain a total of 384 lines.

The termination of one kua is always the beginning of another. For instance, all periods of decrease, Kua 41, "Sun," are followed by periods of increase, Kua 42, "I," and vice-versa. Each of the six lines of the kua is capable of changing to its opposite; broken lines to solid and solid lines to broken, thereby reflecting the changing conditions of the world. If your answer had moving lines, (more on that later), those new conditions are reflected in the next kua, which is made up of the lines of the first kua that did not change and the new lines that did. Each of the sixty-four hexagrams can change into one another through the movement of one or more of the six lines that form the hexagram. There are 4,096 possible combinations (64 × 64) which represent every possible condition in Heaven and on Earth.

Using the I Ching, we can find out what situation or condition exists with regard to any question. By taking the appropriate actions, actions we can discover in the I Ching, we can turn any condition or situation into any other condition or situation. Is that not wonderful? (For a fuller discussion of that process, read this author's books, *The I Ching*, and/or *A Tale of the I Ching*.)

CHAPTER ONE
Does It Work?

The Universe is alive—an aware, conscious entity.

Sometimes we read a sentence in a book and pass on to the next sentence without having fully grasped the meaning of the words we have read. Before passing on to other sentences in this book, I humbly request that you read again and think about the first sentence on this page. It is essential that the words in the first sentence on this page regarding the aliveness of the Universe be fully grasped. If you have already fully grasped their meaning, I apologize for what follows, but since the meaning of the first sentence is the heart and soul underlying the entire divination process as well as our own relationship to the rest of the Universe, I must elaborate, for it is only with the full understanding of those words that we can interact with the Universe at the level that permits the full communication and the intimate relationship possible for us who are part of the Universe.

As we are alive, aware and conscious; able to experience, to create, to do, to think, and to communicate, so is the rest of the Universe. As we are an entity, a being, so is the Universe. What we are, what we can do, are powers derived from the Universe. Since we *are* the Universe, a part of it, you could say that it is the Universe doing those things through us. We are alive because *it* is alive; we can think because *it* can think; we can act because *it* can act. To doubt that would be the same as looking down at your hands playing a piano and saying, "Look at what my hands can do," as if your hands were playing on their own, without the participation of the rest of you. We are the Universe expressing itself and experiencing itself.

It is for that reason that we can know what the Universe knows. It also answers the question, "Does the system work?" The answer is, Yes, it works—perfectly. Every time? Yes, every time. If you think about it, you will realize that it is the only possibility. Let me take a few lines from my interpretation of the I Ching, and reprint them here.

How can you be certain the answers are correct? After you have received an answer to a vitally important question and feel everything within you resonating with the truth, wisdom, and guidance contained in the answer—a resonance so pure and sweet that it brings joy to your heart, and sometimes tears to your eyes— you will, at that moment, be certain that the question was perfectly answered, divinely answered. At those moments you can experience your oneness with All-That-Is. Having had the experience, you will never again wonder who it is or what it is answering your questions or whether the answers are correct.

Can the answers be confusing or difficult to interpret? Not if the question is phrased correctly and is an appropriate question for you to ask. For instance, if you are using the I Ching to ask too many questions, thereby not relying on your own intellect and intuition sufficiently, the answers will be confusing. The reason is that the Universe will not allow you to rely on it exclusively to run your life. It is a guide, an infallible guide, but only to your betterment, never to your detriment. Two examples of inappropriate questions are: asking about your neighbor out of idle curiosity with no real need for the information; asking about the outcome of a situation that does not concern you. Answers to that type of question will generally appear confusing. If an answer you receive is unclear or confusing, it will always be because the question was not phrased correctly, such as asking two or three questions in one, using the I Ching too much, or asking questions not pertinent to your life, or appropriate for you to ask, or for some other similar reason.

How do you know the difference between an answer you can totally rely on and one which you can't? If the answer fits the question perfectly, such as the examples you will find later in this book, you can rely on it completely. If the answer is without reference or significance to your question, you are either asking incorrectly, asking too many questions, or asking an inappropriate question. If you are using any method of divination other than yarrow stalks, the answer may appear correct, and in some cases, may be correct, but my own experience has proven to me that only the yarrow stalk method is completely reliable.

When you hold the yarrow stalks in your left hand, think of your question, and, with your right hand grasp a number of stalks from the bundle in your left hand, you have exceeded the capacity of your rational mind to know how many stalks you have grasped. You have crossed the boundary of rational thinking and entered into the purely spiritual world where everything is known. In grasping and counting eighteen times, you build up the kua from the bottom and so peer into the future, or if you like, into the past. You can receive guidance in designing your own future development and, through the Universal law of cause and effect, create for yourself a future of peaceful prosperity and harmony. Is that not wonderful?

CHAPTER TWO
How It Works

Within certain limitations you have free will. An example of such a limitation is not being able to alter the past; once you have crushed the eggshell under your heel, you cannot undo the action. Even if you were able to perfectly reconstruct the eggshell, it would not alter what you did to it originally.

You can expose yourself to beneficial forces or destructive forces; that is one of the best uses of the I Ching. However, when you get an answer to an I Ching reading that foretells success, it does not mean that success is inevitably forthcoming. Your actions from the time of reading the answer until the result is achieved determines the success or failure of your efforts. An example will help to clarify what I am saying.

Suppose you were thinking of running for public office and did a reading to determine what the outcome of the election would be. Let's say that you asked the question, "What can I expect as a result of running for the office of mayor of my town?" Let's say that the answer was Kua 19,

Lin, Advance, and that there were no moving lines in your answer. The text of Kua 19 reads:

> During this propitious time, your advance will be crowned with supreme success. You must act swiftly and make the best use of the time, for the time of rapid, easy advance does not last forever. The ancient text reads that the superior man is inexhaustible in his teaching and that his tolerance of the people and his protection of them knows no limits.

According to your reading, the result of your efforts will be "crowned with supreme success." However, if you take that to mean that no matter what you do you will be supremely successful, you may miss the mark completely and lose the election by a wide margin. You are instructed to "act swiftly and make the best use of the time." If, instead of acting swiftly and entering the race for mayor, you take an extended vacation, you will most likely experience a dismal failure rather than a supreme success.

An actual example occurred a few years ago when a teacher, Hank, was being interviewed for a job. He had done a reading and received kua 19 as an answer. There were no moving lines. He went on the interview full of confidence, thinking he would be "supremely successful" but was not hired for the position. He was amazed because his reading had indicated "Supreme success." When he told me what had happened at the interview, it was clear why he had experienced the failure. During the interview, Hank didn't say much and was just waiting for the interview to end. At the end of the interview, the prospective employer told Hank he would call him when he had made his decision. Hank, thinking about the answer he had received, replied in a boastful manner, "I already know the outcome, and I'll be ready for work next week." His overbearing immodesty ruined what could have been a successful interview.

The message of this chapter is that the answers we get using the I Ching are based on the assumption that we will carefully follow the guidance provided by the reading. We should ponder the answers, sifting through them for the gems of wisdom they contain, and then we should keep their counsel uppermost in our minds as we proceed toward our goals. The future that unfolds will be a result of our past, present and future actions, and, by taking the appropriate actions, we can enjoy a future of success and good fortune. Failing that, we will experience a future of despair and hardship.

CHAPTER THREE

The Language of the Universe

We are constantly communicating with that being that is the Universe, some of us knowingly, others of us unknowingly, and the Universe is constantly communicating with us. We use words, thoughts, and actions to speak to the Universe, and the Universe uses events to speak to us. Events are the language of the Universe.

Once we fully grasp that concept, our lives take on a meaning and a potential that makes all that has gone before pale into insignificance and brightens our future in limitless ways. We become happier, more confident, and less afraid because of our knowledge. We consciously become partners with the Universe, actually, an extension of it. We are partners with the Universe even without that knowledge, but having the knowledge makes a difference that raises the level of our existence to the sublime. Sublime, as used here, means lofty, godlike.

The most basic law of our Universe is "cause and effect." Stated, the law says, "Every action produces a result, and the result is in perfect accord with the action." In the physical world, a pebble thrown into a pond produces ripples; the bigger the pebble, the bigger the ripples. In the metaphysical world, the way we are being at every moment influences everyone and everything around us and determines our future. A continually angry person will soon drive away all his friends and reap an unfriendly response from his associates. Seeing ourselves as part of the Universe causes us to act in a manner that enhances our lives and brings us incomparable benefits.

We produce effects in the Universe by being the way we are at every moment: happy, sad, generous, miserly, aware, unaware, loving, angry, etc. The responses we receive as a result of our actions are communications from the Universe. Thinking in those terms is difficult at first, and it takes perseverance to maintain that awareness, but the task becomes easier as we keep at it and come to understand the language of the Universe.

To increase the quality of our communication with the Universe, we need only acknowledge the Universe whenever an obvious communication occurs. For instance, if we are expecting an important telephone call and are away from the telephone for almost the entire day, but receive the call during the one time we are near the telephone for a few minutes, acknowledging the Universe in some way such as with a knowing smile or quietly saying, "Thanks," is enough and will result in greatly improved and more frequent obvious communications. I use the word "obvious" because although the Universe is constantly communicating with us, as we are with it, we are not always aware of the communication. Some of the communications are more obvious than others and those are the ones we become aware of. On those occasions when we become aware of a communication, we should acknowledge the Universe. Taking that action will result in an ever-broadening, ever deepening level of communication and will bring us benefits that are wondrous indeed. The more time we spend being aware of our role in the Universe, the easier it becomes to maintain the awareness that we *are* the Universe, a part of it. After a time, a time which is different for each of us, we can spend our days consciously being aware of the communication. That is a wondrous time indeed.

CHAPTER FOUR

The Continuation of the Universe and Us

The Universe wants to continue to exist. That is obvious to us all. Perhaps I should not say that it is obvious to us all that the Universe "wants" anything, but I have, and I apologize to you if you believe that we live in a dead, unresponsive Universe. I have written more extensively on that topic in an earlier book, *I Ching Life*. In any case, the laws that govern the operation of the Universe provide for its continuation.

We can see that favorable inclination of the Universe to continue reflected in the mathematical probabilities inherent in the yarrow stalk divination process. The chances of getting a nine, which is a favorable, light giving, powerful line, are three in sixteen. The chances of getting a six, which is a weak, dark, unfavorable line, are one in sixteen. That means that the chances of getting a favorable nine are three times greater than those of getting an unfavorable six. (Note: To those of you who use coins in the divination process, the chances of getting a six or a nine are equal, which is the main reason that yarrow stalks should be used rather than coins. A more extensive discussion of the coin oracle and the yarrow stalk oracle can be found in this author's book, *The I Ching*.)

That is not to say that all broken lines forebode ill fortune and all solid lines predict good fortune, for each can reveal either good or ill depending on the kua in which it appears and on its position within the kua. There will be more on that in a later chapter.

The great sage, Fu Hsi, who conceived of the yarrow stalk method of divination thousands of years ago, understood that the Universe was heavily weighted toward favorability, toward continuation, and he built that favorability into the yarrow stalk divination method.

CHAPTER FIVE
A Letter to the Universe

When we use the I Ching to ask a question, it's as if we are writing a letter to the Universe. It's something like this:

Dear Universe:

I would like to know what I can expect as a result of taking on a new line of work as a salesperson. Please tell me.

Sincerely,

A Seeker.

We then manipulate the yarrow stalks and the resulting kua is our answer.

The answers come from the consciousness of the Universe, and because the Universe benefits itself in the maximum way at all times, and since we *are* the Universe, a part of it, the answers we get are always for our highest and best good. Learning to trust the answers, which is learning to trust the Universe, may take some time, but it is the most worthwhile and rewarding undertaking of which I know.

ABOUT THIS
NEWLY REVISED EDITION

Since I wrote the original version of this book in 1997, I have published a newly revised edition of the *I Ching: The Book of Answers* that has changed the text considerably. I have retained the original text for the stories within this book because it was the book that the participants were using when the events occurred. I have also added several new short stories to the book to show how the readings can be used where only one reading is necessary.

part two

THE READINGS

Over the course of many years I have had the opportunity and great pleasure of working with many people who sought guidance using the I Ching. The great trust they placed in me by disclosing their innermost thoughts and feelings and in revealing their most private problems caused me to come into possession of the information in this chapter. I like to hear from the people I have guided in the use of the I Ching, and, in some cases, the communication has spanned many years, sometimes decades. I have also come to know some of the people about whom the readings were done, and so I discovered what later happened to them as a result of following or not following the guidance contained in their readings, and what were their private thoughts. With their permission, I humbly offer this information to you for your consideration.

The Well

Sam, a Hollywood film maker, was part of a group that I taught to use the I Ching about fifteen years ago. We kept in close contact for about five years; then I did not hear from him for about ten years. When I did hear from him, it was a telephone conversation asking to meet. At the meeting, Sam told me the painful details of the story you are about to read. He had kept careful notes and copies of all of his readings. I also talked with his son, Mike, who had also kept copies of his readings. Mike recounted for me the emotional turmoil and mental upset he experienced as the events herein unfolded. They thoughtfully provided me with copies of their notes and readings for inclusion in this book.

Sam and Mike had years ago made plans to co-author books and screenplays and to produce movies together. Mike is now twenty years old and in his first year of college. He is majoring in film production and screen writing, and four years earlier he had learned from his father, Sam, how to use the I Ching. They had discussed many of each other's readings, and both of them were serious I Ching students. Sam and Mike have an unusually close relationship and each has great love and respect for the other.

At the beginning of the calendar year before last, when this story begins, Mike did an I Ching reading, as he did each year, asking, "What does the new year hold in store for me?" The answer was Kua 58, Tui, Joyousness—Pleasure. Because Tui is one of the eight kua made up of doubled trigrams, it means that the advice given is to be given extra consideration and is to be strictly followed. Kua 58 reads:

> The main difference between joy and pleasure is that joy comes from within while pleasure comes from without. Joy stems from powerful feelings of contentment and well being; pleasure stems from mental or physical sensory gratification from outside sources. This kua shows that joy comes from inner strength and from following a correct path, and that pleasure, carried to extremes, is injurious. The symbols of this kua are two lakes, one above the other, each feeding the other. The symbol of the lakes is characterized by joy; therefore, it is joy replenishing joy. Providing joy leads to the idea of people joining together for discussion of the great truths of life, thereby nurturing each other. Perseverance on the path of the superior person will lead to joyous success.

There were two moving lines, Line 3 and the top line. The text of Line 3 reads:

> You are in a strong position, but are weak willed. You are not strong enough to resist the temptations of great pleasure and, therefore, will suffer misfortune.

The top line reads:

> Because of your weak nature, you have been unable to withstand the temptation of seductive pleasure. Your yielding can only have unfortunate consequences.

The two moving lines caused Kua 58 to became Kua 1 which reads:

> This is the kua of creating yourself as an individual or creating something of which you conceive. Enormous potential exists here. Follow the six steps of creation as indicated in the lines below to achieve the greatest possible success and to avoid failure. Since all the lines of the kua are strong, light-giving, good lines, perseverance in a virtuous course of action is essential. For acting in accordance with that

**which is highest and best within you, sublime
success that comes from the primal depths of the
Universe is assured. Great good fortune.**

At the time of the reading, Mike had no idea what were the "temptations" and "great pleasures" to which the reading was referring, but he assumed that he would find out during the course of the year, and as usual, he pinned the reading to his wall so he would be occasionally reminded of its counsel. Unfortunately for Mike, he didn't remember the reading when he tried heroin for the first time. No one who tries heroin knows about its deadly addictiveness or they wouldn't do it. Mike thought he could try it once and quit, but once led to twice, twice to three times, and three times to addiction. He tried to quit, but the withdrawal symptoms were too sickening and he couldn't do it. He went to several clinics for help, but to no avail.

Mike was afraid to tell his father about his addiction because he did not want his father to lose respect for him. In their weekly telephone conversations, Mike kept his painful secret and fell into ever greater despair.

Over several months he incurred a great amount of credit card debt, he owed money to all his friends, his bank account was heavily overdrawn, and he was in danger of failing several subjects in school. After a few months the bank canceled his account, and the credit card companies canceled his cards and began legal proceedings to collect the money owed to them. He finally had no choice but to tell Sam about his addiction and his circumstances.

Sam was amazed that Mike had become addicted to heroin. He couldn't understand how Mike, who was very intelligent and knowledgeable, could allow himself to be caught in such a trap, but he never became angry, and he was completely understanding of Mike's problem. Sam agreed to help Mike quit the drug. He stayed with Mike constantly during the first four days of the withdrawal period which Mike said was the most difficult part. They went to movies, an activity they both loved, rented videos to watch at home, walked on the beach, hiked in the hills, went shopping for groceries, and sometimes Sam would read screenplays to Mike. He paid Mike's debts and helped him to organize his life again.

They both agreed that Mike had to find a new circle of friends and to get away from the area, so they searched for and found a new college a few hundred miles away from their house. Mike enrolled in the school and Sam helped him move in.

Two weeks after Mike began classes at the new college his desire to use heroin came back very strong, and he gave in to it. In a brief time, he was addicted to it again. Mike didn't say anything to Sam, he was too embarrassed to do that, and in their telephone conversations, he made believe everything was going well at the new school. Mike was soon in debt again, he was failing a subject, and he owed money to many of his new schoolmates. He had also written a number of bad checks and his checking account was seriously overdrawn.

Mike knew that if he didn't tell Sam about his addiction, he would soon be in trouble he couldn't get out of. One night he called Sam and told him he was back on heroin. Sam had a hard time reconciling himself to the fact that Mike had gone back to the drug after he had once gotten off of it, and he didn't know what to do. The most difficult aspect of the situation for Sam was Mike's deception. Sam had asked Mike several times during the early part of the school year if he was staying away from heroin, and Mike had assured him he was. Sam felt a great sadness knowing that the trust between them was gone, that their relationship had altered, and that he had lost the wonderful, close relationship they had always shared. He was deeply wounded by Mike's betrayal. Mike blamed it on the drug. Sam didn't say anything to Mike because he didn't want to make it any harder on him than it already was, but inside he was hurting.

Sam went to an organization that specialized in teaching parents of addicts how to help their children. He learned about "tough love," meaning that sometimes you must let a person you love suffer the full consequences of his acts rather than help him, and Sam loved Mike enough to let him suffer if it would help him in the end.

Sam got out his *I Ching* and his yarrow stalks and made an inquiry. Sam's question was "What can I do to help Mike with his drug addiction?" The answer was Kua 48, Ching, The Well. The kua reads:

The Well is the symbol of the unchangeable, inexhaustible abundance of the Universe. It is the spiritual source of nourishment and wisdom from which all can draw. In individual situations, the source can stand for a well, a government, a teaching, information, a person or group, or any object under consideration which is a source. If those who draw from the source draw an insufficient amount, or if they fail in their efforts, misfortune results. The superior person encourages others to draw from the source and urges them to help one another in drawing from it.

Sam wrote out his interpretation of the counseling of Kua 48. He wrote: "I should be unchangeable, inexhaustible, and abundant, as is the Universe. I should be the spiritual source from which Mike can draw. If Mike draws an insufficient amount, misfortune. If he draws a sufficient amount, great good fortune. I should encourage Mike to draw from me." In the reading, Lines 4 and 5 were moving lines.

Line 4 reads:

The source is undergoing purification. During the
purification, the source is not available for use, but
afterward it will be better than before. No blame
will attach to him who does the purifying for having
rendered the source unavailable during the purification process.

With regard to Line 4 Sam wrote: "Mike is undergoing
purification. He is not himself during this time and is not
able to be useful to himself or anyone else. Later, he will not
incur blame for having undergone the purification process
and for not being available to help himself or others during the purification process.

Line 5 reads:

Here, in the place of the leader, the source is pure and
readily available so that everyone can be nourished."

With regard to Line 5, Sam wrote: "Because Line 5 comes
after Line 4 in time, there will come a time when Mike will
have finished the purification process, and he will be pure
and able to help himself and others. He will actually be better and stronger than before."

The changing lines, 4 and 5, resulted in a new Kua, 32, Hêng, Duration. Hêng reads:

Enduring in the face of obstacles, pain, fatigue, frustration, opposition, hardship, and even enduring in good times will all bring you success. To begin anew at every ending, to cultivate long lasting virtues, to develop constancy, will all bring you success. Acting with endurance relieves you of all blame. Having goals and lofty aims will benefit you. The superior person stands firm in the changing times and does not change his direction.

Because Sam's question was what to do about Mike, Sam understood that even though Mike's purification process might be long and hard, even though Mike might slip back into heroin again, Sam was to be the unchangeable, inexhaustible, abundant spiritual source of nourishment and wisdom from which Mike could draw. He was to be "The Well."

Sam took Mike home from school. He again sat with Mike through the withdrawal period. They again went to movies, watched videos, walked on the beach, hiked in the hills, ate their meals together, and, within a week, Mike said that he felt strong enough to go back to school and to stay away from heroin.

In a final conversation at the airport, Sam told Mike that each of us has a personal relationship with the Universe and that the situation Mike was in was between Mike and his Universe. He said that he believed that it was the intention of the Universe to always benefit itself, and since Mike was part of the Universe, and not acting in a manner that was beneficial to himself, the Universe would most likely step in and take some type of corrective action. The action would not be to punish Mike—Sam didn't believe the Universe worked like that—but to instruct him, to correct him and put his feet back on a proper path. That didn't mean that the action wouldn't feel like punishment, but that punishment wasn't the goal, just the means. He also said that the Universe didn't fool around, and that the corrective action would perfectly fit the situation, not too severe, and not too mild, but a lesson that would bring the point strongly home.

Sam also said that if Mike couldn't overcome his addiction, his addiction would overcome him. There was no possibility of a compromise. Mike promised he would keep straight.

Sam was happy and sad. He was happy that Mike was making an effort to stay straight, but he was sad that his relationship with Mike had changed. He also knew that very few heroin addicts are able to stay away from the drug for a lifetime. He saw the treasure of his life, his only son, becoming overwhelmed by heroin addiction. He saw all the great plans that he and Mike had made to write books and go into movie-making together evaporating.

Back at school, Mike did an I Ching reading. His question was: "What do I need know about my situation with regard to heroin?" The answer was Kua 44, Kou, Return of the Dark Force. Kua 44 reads:

After an absence, the dark force, which is represented by the broken line at the bottom, returns suddenly and unexpectedly. The dark force comes in the form of a dangerous temptation or a person who is either evil-minded or will in some way be a bad influence and cause harm. If the dark force is a woman, she is too powerful and should not be allied with in any way. If the dark force is a man, even though he seems innocuous, he should not be given any power or allied with in any way. To counteract the dark force, you should enact sound policies and practices and should spread them throughout the family, group, organization, state, or country.

Mike read Kua 44 and was amazed at how the reading hit directly at the situation, and he was afraid. He knew that "Return of the dark force" meant that heroin was coming back into his life and it was up to him to resist it. The first two times he had become addicted to heroin he had gotten carried away with it and smoked too much, but he believed that if he just had it once in a while, he could control it. He loved the high it gave him, the wonderful feeling that he was a perfect being, that he could think so clearly, that he was in control of everything. When he went to class high, he was at the height of good feeling. He felt as if he were witty, smart, and everything around him was flowing smoothly. Of course, he realized it was only his illusion, but now he was finished with it. Or was he? According to his reading, it was coming back.

In the reading, Line 4 was a moving line. Line 4 reads:

You are in a trusted position but have a desire to yield to a dangerous temptation. Do not give in to the desire, but maintain your good relationship with your subordinates, and all will be well. Failing in that, you will incur misfortune.

Mike resolved that he would not give in to the temptation when it appeared. He knew that if he was overcome by the heroin once again he could lose his relationship with his father, he could get into trouble with his friends for not paying them back, he could go to jail for the bad checks he knew he would write, and he could be embarrassed on campus by being known as a heroin addict. He had kept his secret from all but his most trusted friends.

Because of the moving line, Kua 44 became 57, Sun—
Gently Penetrating. Kua 57 reads:

> The attributes of this kua, which is formed by the
> doubling of a trigram, are gentleness and ceaseless
> penetration of the mist that cloaks the situation.
> Change is brought about not as the result of a
> great force but because of the unremitting nature
> of a gentle force that penetrates the cloaking mist
> to expose the heart of the situation. It will benefit
> you at this time to have a goal, to seek advice from
> a qualified person or leader, to communicate his
> wishes broadly, and to complete his undertakings.
> Success comes through what is small: achieving
> minor goals, paying attention to details, using minor
> players, practicing modesty.

Mike said that when he read the text of Kua 57 he was
not sure exactly what it meant. He didn't think there was any
mist surrounding the situation. He had been a heroin addict, it was over, and that was that. It wasn't misty at all.

If Mike had asked me to interpret the reading, I would have
told him that anyone who is committing self-destructive acts,
such as using heroin, has a reason for doing so. Most often the
reason is not obvious, but exists below the level of everyday

consciousness, influencing our actions. What Mike was missing in the reading was that he was being told that there was a reason he was using heroin, and that he could discover what the reason was by gently penetrating to the heart of the situation. It was saying that he was on the self-destructive path of heroin, not actually to destroy himself, nor to enjoy the high that heroin gave him, but to accomplish some other purpose of which he was not consciously aware. The counsel given in the reading to seek advice from a qualified person was directing him to a therapist, a counselor, a psychiatrist, or some other qualified person who could uncover the reason he was on the self-destructive path.

To discover the reason behind any self-destructive act, we can look to see what the act accomplishes or is on its way to accomplishing. For instance, suppose Mike hated school and was only going to please his father. Suppose as a result of his use of heroin, he was expelled from school. It might not be obvious to anyone that Mike had become an addict to stop going to school, but a person trained to look for such a cause might be able to discover it. Once Mike was out of school, he would be able more easily to stop the use of heroin because the underlying need for its use had been removed.

In Mike's case, what was being lost was his relationship with his father. Perhaps Mike didn't want to be a writer or work in film; perhaps his father had been putting too much pressure on Mike to prepare himself for a life of working with him; perhaps what Mike needed was to get out from under his father's control and to live his own life, choosing his own career and his own path. Mike's reading was exactly on target, but Mike didn't understand what the reading was telling him, and so he didn't follow the instruction to seek qualified help nor did he attempt to get to the bottom of what was causing his addiction.

The next night Mike was in town and he bumped into one of the two dealers from whom he got his heroin. The dealer asked why he hadn't seen Mike for a while. He asked if Mike was not using heroin any more. Mike replied that he was not using heroin, that it was too expensive and he couldn't afford it. The dealer saw that he was losing a good customer and offered to give Mike some heroin for free. At first, Mike protested, but by the end of the evening he gave in. The dark force had returned.

This time, Mike resolved, it was going to be different. This time, he would just do it once a week. He would keep his usage under control. He would have the best of all possible worlds.

The same night that Mike went to town and met the heroin dealer, Sam also did a reading. He needed to know how Mike would hold his resolve to stay away from heroin. Sam's question was: "How will Mike fare with regard to his battle with heroin?" Sam also received as an answer Kua 44, Kou, Return of the Dark Force, which reads:

After an absence, the dark force, which is represented by the broken line at the bottom, returns
suddenly and unexpectedly. The dark force comes
in the form of a dangerous temptation or a person
who is either evil-minded or will in some way be a
bad influence and cause harm. If the dark force is
a woman, she is too powerful and should not be
allied with in any way. If the dark force is a man,
even though he seems innocuous, he should not
be given any power or allied with in any way. To
counteract the dark force, you should enact sound
policies and practices and should spread them
throughout the family, group, organization, state
or country.

Sam got a shiver up his spine when he read the text of
Kua 44 and he had a bad feeling in the pit of his stomach.
"So," he thought, "the dark force is coming back." The read-
ing had a moving line, 6. Line 6 reads:

You have withdrawn from the situation in an attempt to avoid the dark force, but you have failed.
When the meeting does take place, your aggressive
attitude leads to embarrassment. However, since
your intentions are good and no real contact is
made, no blame attaches to you.

After reading the text of Line 6, Sam knew that Mike was going to be addicted to heroin again. In his notes he wrote that he had withdrawn from the situation so Mike could gain the strength from dealing with his addiction on his own, but apparently Mike had failed or was going to fail. So as to not embarrass himself or Mike, he resolved not to be too aggressive in his response to Mike if he used heroin again.

As a result of the moving line, Kua 44 became Kua 28, Ta Kuo, Excess. The text reads:

This kua depicts a situation in which too much power is being wielded and too many excesses are being indulged in. Too much of anything causes imbalances. Universal law, which is the great equalizer, then causes falling, sagging, or breaking or employs other means for reducing power or excess. If there is anything you can do to moderate the use of power and reduce the excesses, good fortune will be yours. The lower trigram, Sun, indicates that gentleness is to be used in reducing the excess, and the upper trigram, T'ui, indicates that you are to be joyful.

When Sam read the part about too many excesses being indulged in, he knew Mike was in trouble or was soon going to be in trouble. He called Mike at once and asked him how he was doing. Mike said "Fine." They talked for a while and Sam told Mike to call him immediately if he needed any help. Mike said he would. Sam told Mike of his reading and told him to be on his guard, that the temptation to use heroin was going to come back at him and if he gave in to it, the Universe would most likely come down on him and hard. Mike promised to be careful.

The next day Mike was sitting in his room doing homework when the desire to get high came on strongly. Mike kept his heroin in a drawer and several times that afternoon he went to the drawer and opened it and took out the heroin and looked at the black, tarry substance. Each time he put it back, telling himself that he was going to stay off it for a week. By dinner time he had tricked himself into believing it was okay to just do it once more, and then he'd be off it for a week. Of course, as the week passed, Mike used heroin every day. He began borrowing money again; he sold his $400 mountain bike for $100, his Walkman radio for $10, his $1,200 stereo for $200, his $400 TV for $75, and the computer he used to do his homework for $500. The computer had cost his dad $2,500. At the end of two months he was writing bad checks all over town and he owed money to the two heroin dealers who were putting pressure on him.

Mike didn't know how long he could keep going. He knew that he was in danger of going to jail for all the bad checks he was writing, and the heroin dealers were known to be tough guys who beat up users who couldn't pay the money they owed.

Mike did a reading. The answer was Kua 51, Chên, Shock—The Arousing. The kua reads:

Shock! A manifestation of God. It usually causes fear and trembling, but the superior person does not let the shock drive from his mind the awareness that he is a divine creature in a divine Universe and that the shock was entirely for his benefit. He retains his reverence for All-That-Is. Such reverence brings success. After sustaining a shock, the superior person examines his life to see whether he is a good person and accomplishing good things. He then orders his life according to the highest principles.

Mike didn't like the sound of that at all. He knew of two other people who had gotten readings of "Shock." One was later in a severe car accident and lost an arm; the other had later fallen from a cliff and was nearly killed. There was a moving line, 4. It reads:

You are strong, but you are in a bad position, surrounded by inferior people. Thus, when a shock comes, you are unable to make a decisive move. It is like being stuck in deep mud.

He knew what that meant. He had tried to quit, but the withdrawal was too difficult. He needed help and didn't know where to turn for it. He was ashamed and afraid to call his father. Mike was really scared. He went to look for one of the heroin dealers to try and put him off until he figured out a way to get some more money. While he was looking for the dealer, the other dealer to whom he owed money saw him and called him over to his car. Mike had a bad feeling, but he went. The dealer told him to get in his car. Mike got in and the dealer drove him a ways out of town and stopped. He got out of the car and told Mike to do the same. Then he demanded his money. Mike told him he didn't have it but he was going to get it. The dealer's face became a mask of hatred and he punched Mike over the eye so hard that Mike fell to the ground, stunned. Then the dealer began to kick Mike in the face with his boot. Mike knew he was in deep trouble when he heard his jaw bone crack. Mike dragged himself to his feet after the dealer left and made his way back to school. His classmates drove him to the emergency ward of the hospital where his jaw was x-rayed. A maxio-facial surgeon was called in to examine the x-rays, and he told Mike his jaw was broken in two places, including the hinge, and it would have to be wired shut for six weeks. It was going to cost $3,000, and Mike would have to live on liquids, straining them through his teeth. At that point, Mike was in extreme pain, he had no money, and he had no choice but to call Sam.

Sam was angry when he got the phone call. At first, Sam wanted to go and find the dealer and kill him. Then, after he thought about it, he wanted to go and find the dealer and thank him. That's just what his son needed to help him get off heroin, a broken jaw, wired shut for six weeks. Even though Sam had resolved not to respond aggressively, he told Mike he was angry with him, that this was between Mike and his Universe. It didn't involve him. Mike was going to have to suffer all the consequences the Universe was going to dish out for him, including paying the doctor, paying his bad check debts, paying the dealers, and paying his friends. If he went to jail for his bad checks, well, he would have to suffer through it.

Mike worked out a payment plan with the doctor and got his jaw wired shut. He spent days on the phone calling everyone he was indebted to, making arrangements to pay them from the small paycheck he received every two weeks for working in the school gym.

When Mike did that first reading at the beginning of the year to find out what the year held in store for him, the kua into which his situation changed was Kua 1. The text of Kua 1 reads:

This is the kua of creating yourself as an individual or creating something of which you conceive. Enormous potential exists here. Follow the six steps of

creation as indicated in the lines below to achieve
the greatest possible success and to avoid failure.
Since all the lines of the kua are strong, light-giving,
good lines, perseverance in a virtuous course of action is essential. For acting in accordance with that
which is highest and best within you, sublime success that comes from the primal depths of the Universe is assured. Great good fortune.

Mike had read those words, but he didn't take heed of
the counsel and follow through. For the most part, the counsel given in the *I Ching* is to be taken literally and acted on
precisely. Mike's course of action led directly to the consequences described in this narrative.

There is a point I wish to make at this time because it is
relevant to Mike's situation and because it is also one of the
most important points in knowing how to respond to the
counsel we receive using the *I Ching*. Mike read at the beginning of the year in Kua 1 "sublime success that comes from
the primal depths of the Universe is assured." The point is that
the reading did not mean that sublime success was assured
under any and all circumstances, but that the sublime success
would come only if Mike followed the counsel given in the
reading to persevere in a virtuous course of action.

After Mike's teeth were wired tightly together, he called and
asked his father if he had done a reading to see how he should

be reacting to Mike. Sam said no, he hadn't and didn't want to, that Mike was on his own.

Sam felt very bad. He was hurting physically, spiritually, and mentally. It was as if he had lost his best friend. He and Mike were always close, real pals, and to think that the relationship was over left Sam with an empty feeling. He couldn't work, he lost weight, he couldn't sleep, and he was in a constant rage. He didn't know what he was in a rage about; it wasn't Mike; it wasn't the Universe; it wasn't anything he could put his finger on. He just felt empty and mad. And he wouldn't do a reading.

When I asked Sam why he hadn't done a reading to get some guidance, he said that he just didn't want to. He believed Mike was going to have to work his problems out with the Universe and that was that. But, as you will read, the Universe has its own way of communicating when it wants to, whether we do a reading or not.

A day or two later Sam was sorting through his papers when one of them fell to the floor. He picked it up and saw that it was the I Ching reading he had done when Mike had become addicted to heroin for the second time. The question had been, "What should I do about Mike?" The answer had been Kua 48, Ching, The Well. He read what he had written on his paper as a conclusion: "I should be unchangeable, inexhaustible, and abundant, as is the Universe. I should be the spiritual source from which Mike can draw."

Because of its moving lines, that kua had turned into Kua 32, Hêng, Duration. Sam read once again the counsel of Kua 32:

> Enduring in the face of obstacles, pain, fatigue, frustration, opposition, hardship, and even enduring in good times will all bring you success. To begin anew at every ending, to cultivate long lasting virtues, to develop constancy, will all bring you success. Acting with endurance relieves you of all blame. Having goals and lofty aims will benefit you. The superior person stands firm in the changing times and does not change his direction.

Sam remembered his resolve at that time, that even though Mike's purification process might be long and hard, even though Mike might slip back into heroin again, he, Sam, was going to be the unchangeable, inexhaustible, abundant spiritual source of nourishment and wisdom from which Mike could draw. He was to be "The Well."

Seeing that reading, and remembering his resolve, Sam called Mike immediately and told him he was on his way to see him, that everything was all right.

Mike had a friend drive him to the airport where he met Sam at the plane. They embraced warmly and spent the day together. Sam was shocked when he saw how thin Mike was and how awful he looked with all the wires on his teeth and listened to him speak through immovable jaws. Sam told me that Mike looked like something out of a science fiction movie.

Mike told Sam the whole story about how he had become addicted again, about his belief that he was stronger than heroin, and how he had thought that he could do it once a week and control it. Sam asked Mike if he still believed that. Mike said it had been a ridiculous idea, that he now knew he had just tricked himself into believing that so he could have more heroin. He told Sam that he was finished with it forever, that he knew that it was impossible for him to just have it once and then quit. If he had it once, he was hooked.

Sam felt wonderful. He knew he should be doubtful, that he should take Mike out of school and put him in a program, but no matter what had happened in the past, he still believed in Mike. He said he knew that he would be thought stupid in the eyes of anyone hearing the story, but he had complete faith in Mike. Besides, it hurt him too much to treat Mike as though he didn't care for him. He just couldn't do it. He felt as if he had gotten back his son. His depression lifted, and he began to feel like his old self. Before he left to return home, he reminded Mike that it was the Universe that had kicked his jaw; it was just using the booted foot of the drug dealer. Mike said he understood that, and said that even when he was lying on the ground after he was kicked and beaten, he looked up and smiled at the Universe, and said, "Okay, I got the message." It was that kind of remark that endeared Mike to Sam. He knew that Mike had the information about the ways in which the Universe worked, and he knew that Mike was not a fool.

Just before Sam got on the plane that morning he told Mike something that is of great importance to us all. He said that the Universe has an endless supply of "bad stuff" to dish out when it finds it necessary. What he meant was that when we are "off the path," meaning when we're not doing what we're supposed to be doing, the Universe communicates that to us with an event. When we are "off our paths," doing things that are bad for us, the event is a bit of misfortune, a bit of unpleasantness, something we don't like and wish was not in our lives. It is not meant to punish us, but to communicate to us that we are "off the path." It's a Universal tap on the shoulder.

What Sam was telling Mike, is that the Universe has an endless supply of unpleasantness to dole out if it is needed. It is very like a water faucet which pours forth both good and bad events *that we regulate by our conduct and thoughts.* If we want to bring great good fortune and happiness into our lives, it is only necessary that we do what we're supposed to be doing; that we stay "on the path." What it is that we're supposed to be doing is different for each of us, but each of us knows what it is. We also know when we're doing something that is "off our path." When some unpleasantness comes into your life, you should not be surprised. The information about why it happened is right there, inside of you, and you can change it any moment, including this one, by turning back before you have gone too far.

Sam pointed out to Mike that it was evident that the Universe didn't want him using heroin, and that Mike's wired jaw, which would keep him straining liquids through his teeth for the next six weeks, would be a constant reminder. More importantly, if Mike went back to heroin, the next reminder might be a permanent one; Mike could get a Universal message he'd remember every day for the rest of his life, if such a lesson was needed. Mike said he knew that, and it would not be necessary. This time, he said, he was off it for good. He began the next day to call everyone to whom he was indebted, and to make arrangements to pay them over a period of time. The ones who wouldn't wait, who threatened to have him put in jail, Sam paid. He said he was going to stand by Mike, whatever it took.

A few days later, Mike went to a counselor to discover the underlying reason Mike started using heroin in the first place. At the time of this writing, that's as far as the story goes. Mike is still wearing his wires and has another three weeks to go before they come off.

It would have been beneficial to Mike and Sam if they had done several more readings during the time of Mike's involvement with heroin. Mike also would have benefited if he had referred to his readings more often. Sam should have also done another reading regarding the outcome of Mike's latest effort to overcome his heroin addiction.

I would like to point out that, as you can see from the above narrative, the *I Ching* sometimes states what is going to happen as if we did not have free will. When Mike first made an inquiry about what he could expect from the calendar year, Line 3 specifically stated,

> You are in a strong position, but are weak willed. You are not strong enough to resist the temptations of great pleasure and, therefore, will suffer misfortune."

The top line, which is later in time than Line 3, stated:

> "Because of your weak nature, you have been unable to withstand the temptation of seductive pleasure. Your yielding can only have unfortunate consequences.

It appears from reading Line 3 and the top line, that what Mike eventually went through was inevitable from the outset; as if the Universe had peered into the future and seen what was going to happen and, through the I Ching, had revealed it to Mike. Yet I believe that we have free will, and that we can shape our fates by taking the appropriate action. I believe that even though Mike's reading stated that he would suffer unfortunate consequences, that had he been on the alert and kept aware of the reading, he could have recognized the offering of the heroin as the temptation of "great pleasure" that the I Ching reading alluded to, and he would have refused the heroin, thereby avoiding the misfortune foretold.

Whenever we get an answer that foretells of danger or misfortune, we must be as alert for the source of the danger as a fox walking across a pond on thin ice, or as a hungry hawk looking for prey. In that way, we can avoid the pitfalls of the average person who knows not that danger is near nor what to look for.

You, who are reading this, are a seeker on the path of greatest learning. Ponder what you have read, allow the great wisdom to seep into your innermost being, and you will inexorably rise through the skies of success as though on the wings of six dragons.

Since this story was first written, about eight years have passed. Mike continued to battle his heroin addiction for several years and finally was able to discover the reason he was using heroin. It had to do with his dad. Mike wanted his dad to see him as heroic, as wonderful, as grand as Mike saw his dad, and he despaired of being able to ever reach that goal. Heroin gave him the ability to fantasize that he was all of those grand things. Once he discovered what he was running from and was able to come to terms with it by talking to his dad, he completely recovered and is now engaged in a great profession where he helps people who are suffering from addiction.

The Racer

The following story concerns a young man who I came to know very well. We had several long talks about what happened to him in this story, and so I am privileged to know his innermost thoughts. He was eager for me to share his story with you.

Sean was twenty when he purchased a Japanese racing motorcycle. He loved to drive it, and he loved the thrill of its power. In a short time he received six traffic citations for speeding. After the last one, the Department of Motor Vehicles in his state notified him that if he got one more citation, his license would be suspended for a year. Sean got a citation the next day for speeding—twenty-five miles per hour over the posted maximum speed limit. Sean was worried that he would lose his license for a year, but the real shock came when he went in to pay the ticket and was told by the cashier of the violations division that he was not permitted to just pay the fine and have the citation recorded against his record, but that he had to appear in court and face the judge. The hearing was set for a date four weeks away. She said that the judge dealt very harshly with repeat offenders, and, that because Sean had so many speeding citations and because his current speeding ticket was so far in excess of the speed limit, the odds were that he would have to spend anywhere from a few days to a month in jail. Sean decided to plead not guilty and take his chances in court.

Sean had heard terrible stories of the county jail and what happened to people who were put there. He was terrified. Court was four weeks away, and he knew he would be in a terrible state of mind until then. Fortunately for Sean, he had learned how to use the I Ching. He got out his book and his yarrow stalks and did a reading. His question was, "What can I expect when I go to court on January 31 for my speeding ticket?" The answer was Kua 28, Ta Kuo, Excess of Power. The kua reads:

This kua depicts a situation in which too much power is being wielded and too many excesses are being indulged in. Too much of anything causes imbalances. Universal law, which is the great equalizer, then causes falling, sagging, or breaking or employs other means for reducing power or excess. If there is anything you can do to moderate the use of power and reduce the excesses, good fortune will be yours. The lower trigram, SUN, indicates that gentleness is to be used in reducing the excess, and

the upper trigram, T'ui, indicates that you are to
be joyful."

Sean recognized that the kua perfectly described his situation; he was guilty of great excess in his speeding tickets and the use of too much power with his motorcycle. What worried him about the reading was that now the Universe, the great equalizer, was going to break him to stop the excessive use of power, and he was afraid even though the reading said he was to be joyful.

Sean's reading had a moving line, 4, which reads:

The overuse of power or the excesses that have
been indulged in have caused great imbalance in
your situation, which is now dangerous. However,
help comes from an outside source, even a universal source. It is as if a sagging ridgepole is braced at
its center. Good fortune. It will be embarrassing if
ulterior motives are present."

Sean was elated. Line 4 stated that he was going to be helped, that he would have good fortune. He imagined the image described in Line 4, the sagging ridgepole. He knew that a ridgepole was a pole that horizontally supported a roof at its center line and that it was supported on either end by a brace. In his case, the ridgepole was sagging in the middle because of the excessive weight of all of his traffic citations. It was sagging to the breaking point, and the addition of this last citation could cause the collapse of the whole structure. But there, in Line 4, he was being told that he would be helped. The Universe, in one form or another, was going to place a support under the center of the ridgepole. Good fortune. Sean felt an immense relief knowing that he would be safe. He didn't know in what form his salvation would come, but he had been using the I Ching long enough to know that whatever it was, it was going to save him. Because of the moving line, Kua 28 became Kua 48, Ching, The Well. The text of Kua 48 reads:

> The Well is the symbol of the unchangeable, inexhaustible abundance of the Universe. It is the spiritual source of nourishment and wisdom from which all can draw. In individual situations, the source can stand for a well, a government, a teaching, information, a person or group, or any object under consideration which is a source. If those who draw from the source draw an insufficient amount, or if they fail in their efforts, misfortune results. The superior person encourages others to draw from the source and urges them to help one another in drawing from it.

Sean believed that the reading was telling him that he would receive a great teaching from his experience in going to court. He would wait and see.

Four weeks later Sean went to court. His father went with him. Ordinarily, Sean always told the truth, but he was so afraid of going to jail that he was prepared to lie. He had told his father of his intentions. His dad didn't like the idea of Sean's lying and said so. Sean said he was going to do it anyway if it would prevent his going to jail. Sean's father reminded him what the I Ching says about following the path of the superior person, that one should turn back before going too far with digressions from that path. Sean said that he understood that, but that he was going to lie and testify that he was not speeding if it would save him from going to jail.

When Sean's case was called, the bailiff asked Sean to please step forward into the defendant's box in front of the judge. The judge then addressed the two rows of policemen who were sitting in the jury box waiting to testify on various cases. He asked that the officer who had issued the speeding citation to come forward and be sworn in. There was silence. No movement from the fifteen or twenty police officers in the courtroom. The judge called for the police officer again. Still no answer. The judge looked over at Sean and said, "You're a mighty lucky young man. You were probably on your way to jail. The police officer who gave you the speeding ticket is not in court and I have no choice but to dismiss your case. You may leave. I advise you to slow down."

As they left the courtroom, Sean silently thanked the Universe for his salvation. He also realized what the last part of Line 4 was talking about when it said, "It will be embarrassing if ulterior motives are present." He was embarrassed because he had been afraid and had been prepared to lie and his father knew it. He later told me that he was very dissatisfied with himself for being prepared to lie, even though he knew that the I Ching counsels against it.

Sean realized that as a result of his experience he had become more aware that the Universe truly was alive and aware, and that it knew all things, past, present, and future; that it was in fact, "The Well," the unchangeable, inexhaustible, abundant, spiritual source of complete nourishment and wisdom from which all can draw. How else could it have known that the policeman would not show up? Sean also realized that as a part of the Universe, he too, could be "The Well," and that he should do his part to spread the word.

After Sean returned home from the court hearing, he read Kua 28 again to see if there was anything to which he should be paying attention. One part of the text read:

If there is anything you can do to moderate the use of power and reduce the excesses, good fortune will be yours.

Sean realized there was something he could do. He sold his motorcycle. Now, two years later, Sean reports that he has indeed experienced great good fortune.

Gathering Together

Anita, the woman in this story, has been using the I Ching for twenty-five years. She was shown how to use the I Ching and the yarrow stalks by her grandfather, who had learned in China during World War II. We met in London in 1972 at the Mind, Body, and Spirit exhibition. I had an *I Ching* under my arm which she saw and stopped to talk to me. We struck up a friendship that lasted. Anita provided me with the details of this story to share with you.

Anita owns a book publishing company and does an I Ching reading every year on her birthday. Her question is always the same: "What does my birthday year hold in store for me?" One particular year, the answer was Kua 45, Ts'ui, Gathering Together. There were no moving lines. The text of Kua 45 reads:

> You are called upon either to join a group or gather others into a group. In joining, your motivation should be clear and strong; in gathering a group, your cause must be well-defined, one around

which everyone can gather and which all will support. To achieve a successful end, seek advice from
a qualified person before beginning. Do not slacken
until your objective is reached. You will be called
upon to make sacrifices to obtain your goal. Making
sacrifices is appropriate. Success will be yours.

Anita had no plans either to join a group or cause others to join a group, but she was expectantly looking forward
to the opportunity predicted for her by her reading. As she
did each year, Anita pinned the reading on the book case
over her desk where she would readily see it. Two months
after the reading, Anita moved from her house to another
house. In the bustle of moving, the reading was taken down
and filed but not put back up when the move was completed.

A month or two later, the company that distributed
Anita's books nationwide went bankrupt. In addition to representing Anita, the distribution company represented about
two hundred other publishers. Anita knew that the publishers would scatter, all seeking new representation. She
quickly wrote a letter to all two hundred publishers, asking
them to stay together as a group, and to seek distribution
representation collectively, which would give them a great
deal of power. Many of the publishers who received Anita's
letter called,wrote, or faxed her. She spent days on the phone,
talking until she was hoarse, in her efforts to keep the pub-

lishers together. She also negotiated with the major national distributors to see if there was one who would make a collective deal for all of the publishers that would be a better deal than any of them could make negotiating individually. She found one distributor who was willing to do that, and she passed the information along to the other publishers for their consideration. More phone calls came in and more letters and faxes. Anita was the center for the effort to keep the publishers together.

After two full weeks of calling others, Anita began to feel some urgency to get back to running her own company, which was, indeed, suffering from neglect. She reasoned that she could call the remaining publishers later or send them a quick fax and leave any action up to them. After all, she had accomplished most of her goal. She had done her part, sacrificed enough of her time, energy, and resources to keep many publishers together with the best distribution arrangement possible. She would call one or two others whom she knew well and then look at her own books in progress.

One person she called thanked Anita for her efforts, for pulling the publishers together, for making them into an identifiable group, and for achieving such a remarkable success. The caller added that Anita now certainly deserved to shift her attention away from that effort. Anita especially like hearing those words, and realized she could slacken her efforts. Several hours later, as she was thinking about that, that word "slacken," jogged her memory. Soon, she made the connection, recognizing that the word was from her birthday reading. She took out her I Ching file and reviewed that reading, stopping when she reached the passage:

> **Do not slacken until your objective is reached. You will be called upon to make sacrifices to obtain your goal. Making sacrifices is appropriate. Success will be yours.**

She immediately took up where she had left off, calling the remaining publishers, urging them to stay together. Anita achieved her goal brilliantly. The benefits of her effort are still being felt by everyone, including herself, and she has won the acclaim of her fellow publishers and the gratitude of the new distributor she and her fellow publishers signed with.

The benefits of doing a reading on each birthday and the turn of each new year are impossible to over-estimate. It is a wise course to follow Anita's example. Post your reading in a place where you will see it often. Ask other questions such as, "What can I do to have the best financial year?" "What can I do to have the most successful year in my profession?" "How can I find my mate this year?" "What area of self-improvement will bring me the greatest rewards?" Pin up the sheets of paper where you can see them. Read them over at intervals to see if you are following the advice.

Tongue-Tied

Roy is a very close friend to my son, Pax. They have known each other since childhood, and it was Pax who taught Roy to use the I Ching. Pax told me what Roy had gone through and I talked to Roy at length about what happened to him in the following story.

The day Roy arrived at Ohio State to begin his freshman year he fell in love. Christi was everything he had ever dreamed of in a woman.

Carl. G. Jung, the great Swiss psychiatrist, said that we each carry in our minds the image of our perfect mate. In the man, the image is called the *anima*, in the woman, the *animus*. In the man, the image is most likely made up of his mother's face, the face of his favorite teacher, his grandmother, his favorite baby-sitter, calendar girls he has seen in pictures, billboards depicting beautiful women, his first girlfriends, his first love, and his favorite TV or film stars. In short, the face in his mind is a composite of all the most beautiful and loved women in his life. The same is true for women, in that their image is a composite of the most handsome and most loved men in their lives.

For Roy, the face of Christi fitted his image perfectly. She sent him into a tailspin. When he saw her, he actually lost his breath and his heart started to beat wildly. His jaw hung down, and he could not prevent himself from staring at her as she passed by him on the campus. He was hooked. Walt Disney, in his great film, "Bambi," called it "twitterpated."

Roy spent his first days on campus getting started in college and looking for Christi. He couldn't get her out of his mind. He found out her name, where she lived, where her home town was, her age, her major, everything he could. At unexpected times he came face to face with her, turning a corner, in the library, at the cafeteria, in the bookstore, or coming out of a classroom. Each time he had the same strong physical reaction. He'd lose his breath, his heart would beat wildly, and he would become tongue-tied. He would try to speak to her, but nothing would come out. He could only stare helplessly as she passed him, seemingly unaware of his existence.

Roy did an I Ching reading. His question was, "What do I have to do to have a relationship with Christi?" The answer was Kua 31, Hsien, Attraction, Influence. The kua reads:

The universal force of attraction pulls beings together for every purpose. Coming together is a joyous event and brings great success. Good fortune will attend the forming and formalizing of long lasting relationships. By being perseveringly

modest, receptive, and inviting, and by being devoid
of ulterior motives, you will see your influence grow,
and people will be encouraged to approach you.

Roy was delighted with the overall meaning of the kua.
It was exactly on target. He especially liked the part about the
forming and formalizing of long-lasting relationships and took
it to mean that he would form that kind of relationship with
Christi. He envisioned marriage, a family, and he was elated.
He was determined to follow the reading. He would not en-
tertain any ulterior motives like getting Christi into his bed,
and was sure that as a result Christi would be drawn to him.

There were two moving lines in Roy's reading: the bottom line and the top line. The bottom line reads:

The attraction is in its first stage. Be open and
receptive, and the relationship will develop or not
as a process of natural law.

Roy could not have been more impressed with the accuracy of the reading. He knew the relationship was in its
first stage and resolved to be open and receptive. The top
line reads:

You are attempting to influence people with words
alone. Words can be very powerful when spoken by

the right person at the proper time. Here, the indication is that you do not have the necessary power
or influence to make the words effective.

Roy knew exactly what he was being told. He was trying
to influence Christi with words alone and he did not have
the courage to talk her. He thought he might have to try
something like standing on his head. If he was going to make
any progress, he'd have to find the courage within himself
to speak to her, and maybe he'd have to do more than just
talk. He didn't know what, but he was going to keep thinking about it until he discovered what it was.

As a result of the two moving lines the new kua was 13,
T'ung Jên, Mingling. The kua reads:

This is the kua of people mingling openly. During
this time of mingling, you will benefit if you join
with others or organize others and then undertake
some great endeavor. In fulfilling this achievement,
you must be virtuous in your conduct, and you
must act in the best interests of the group. Your
correct action brings success.

Again, Roy was delighted with his reading. It was a clear
indication that if he found the courage to speak to Christi,
and if he was without ulterior motives, he would be able to

freely associate with her. He joined several college groups, hoping to find Christi in one of them, but without success.

On the rare occasions when he did encounter her, he continued to be tongue-tied. Every few days he'd see her somewhere, and each time he lost his breath, his heart would beat wildly, and he would be unable to speak. He talked to his father about the problem. His father gave him encouragement, and said that it was not unusual to be shy with someone you were powerfully attracted to, but that Roy had to find within himself the courage to overcome his shyness. He urged Roy to speak to Christi. Roy tried, but couldn't. The entire school year passed, and he did not speak one word to her.

At the beginning of the second year, Roy was elated to find Christi in one of his classes that met twice a week. He had spent the summer fantasizing about Christi, and he was sure he'd be able to speak to her that semester. The problem was that nothing had changed. The first day of the class he tried to get up the courage to say something to her, but nothing came out. He was furious with himself. As the days passed, he changed his seat, moving closer and closer to her. When she noticed him, she smiled at him, and he froze. Once, she even lingered at her desk, seeming to wait for him to pass. When he did, she smiled at him invitingly, but he panicked and did not stop. He was beside himself. He didn't know how to proceed.

At the end of the first semester, his father told him he had to leave Ohio State at the end of the next semester and go to a small local college because of a financial set-back in the family. Roy was in despair. He knew the next semester was to be his last chance.

The next semester began, and Christi was not in any of his classes. Neither could he find her anywhere on campus. He did a reading. His question was, "What can I expect from my search for Christi?" The answer was Kua 12, P'i, Separation, Decline. There were no moving lines. Kua 12 reads:

> Inferior people have infiltrated the structure [Roy believed that meant him], and superior people are withdrawing, [Roy thought that meant Christi], which leads to a state of decline. There is but little communication between the superior and the inferior people. ["Little?" thought Roy, "There's none!"] The superior person relies upon his integrity and high moral values to see him through this time of decline and refuses to be tempted into joining with the inferior people, even though they try to bribe him with rewards and riches.

Roy didn't understand the part about the inferior and superior people, nor about the bribery, but he understood about Separation and Decline. He was very despondent.

At the end of the semester, his last at Ohio State, he again found Christi. There was one more day of school left when he saw her walking out of a classroom. He ran over to where she was walking away with a girl friend, but his breath left him, and all his old sensations came back, and again, he couldn't speak to her. He went into the classroom and spoke to the professor. He asked if the class would meet again and was told that they would meet the next day for the last time and take their final exam. Roy checked his watch. The time was five o'clock. He'd be there at four in case she got out early.

Roy was absolutely determined that he would speak to Christi on that last day. He promised himself that he would talk to her no matter what. He planned exactly what he would say, how he would say it, and swore to God that he would do it. He rehearsed his little speech. It wasn't long. It consisted of only one word: "Hello." He knew if he could just say hello, he could then say, "Can I talk to you a minute?"

He did an I Ching reading. His question was: "What can I expect to come from my encounter with Christi tomorrow?" The answer was Kua 25, Wu Wang, Innocent Action, Unexpected Misfortune. Kua 25 reads:

> At birth we are without conscious intention to do good or evil; only when the thought process begins does intent develop. If you remain innocent, acting without ulterior motives, you act in accord with your original nature, and everything works to your advantage, bringing supreme success. If your ac-

tions are not as they should be, you may as well
not attempt anything because the attempt will end
either in failure or a success that you will not enjoy
or ultimately benefit from. This kua also depicts
the condition of unexpected misfortune. If such
befalls you, take heart; it will ultimately work to
your benefit.

Roy had long ago decided to act without ulterior motives and in accord with his original nature. What worried
him was the "unexpected misfortune" part of the reading.
He wondered what that could be. There was a moving line,
Line 4. It reads:

By acting out of your innate goodness, without
thought of gain or reward, you will remain without
blame, and you will make no error.

Good, he was ready to do that. As a result of the moving line, Kua 25 became 42, I, Increase. Kua 42 reads:

You are in a time when everything you do will be
crowned with success and will bring you great gain.
Therefore, you will be benefited if you start toward
some great achievement. You will also be benefited

by far reaching ideas. When the superior person sees good, he imitates it; when he finds faults within himself, he corrects them.

The next day at four o'clock Roy went to the classroom. It was empty except for the professor. Roy's heart sank to his feet and a feeling of despair overcame him. Roy asked the professor where the students were. The professor said the class had met at noon that day to take the final exam, and the last person had left by three. Roy knew then what the unexpected misfortune was.

He also understood the great gain that Kua 42 represents. Roy knew that the lessons he had learned would stand him in good stead for the rest of his life. Never again would he let an opportunity pass him. He would correct his faults, and, as result, he would indeed experience great gain.

Corporate Maneuvering

Although this story took place twenty-five years ago, it seems as relevant today as it was then.

Twenty-five years ago, Barry Bernstein became the president of a large office equipment manufacturing company. He had been with the company for eighteen years, having worked his way up from the mail room. Barry's company made copying machines, telephone answering machines, and other office equipment, but no computer equipment. They were well-equipped to make computers and printers, but the board of directors was dead set against it. Members said that the initial investment was too high, the competition too fierce, and the risk of failure too great for them to take the plunge.

Barry, on the other hand, believed that the future of the company was dependent upon getting into the computer business, and fast. He believed that the business world was going to be dominated by computers and that there was room for many more computer companies. Besides that, the products they currently made were sold in every office machine store in the country and most parts of the world. Distribution was already set up, their name was known, and their entrance into the field would be relatively easy. Furthermore, he believed that if they didn't get into the mainstream of computers immediately, they would be left behind and would slowly diminish in size until they were out of business. As the new president of his company, it was his highest priority to get his company into computer manufacturing.

Barry had been using the *I Ching* since his college days and had relied on it to get where he was in the business world and in his company. It had always served him well, and he treasured his book.

At the time Barry's story begins, he had been president of his company for two months and the next scheduled meeting of the board of directors was one week away. It was to be the first time he would address them as president. Barry had been planning his presentation ever since he took over as president. He believed it was essential for him to convince the directors that the company should expand into computers, and in a major way. Barry got out his *I Ching* and did a reading. His question was, "What should I know about my company to make it more successful?" The answer was Kua 64, Wei Chi, In Order, Out of Place. The text of Kua 64 reads:

> Everything is in order, but out of place. The system, person, group, or item is complete in every detail,

but it is not performing the function for which it was intended or it is not positioned correctly. It may function to some extent, but not efficiently or anywhere near its full potential. Fortunately, everything is only one step away from being in its proper place or being used in its proper function. Therefore, complete success is close, but danger is also close because if extreme caution and good judgment are not exercised, further misplacement will result.

Barry said he was bowled over by the accuracy with which the reading keyed into the situation. It was perfectly clear to him what it was talking about. It was exactly what he believed regarding the expansion of the company into computers. Especially the line that reads:

it is not performing the function for which it was intended . . .

There was a moving line, 3, which reads:

You see the opportunity to make the transition into the proper position by aggressively moving against those who are preventing the transition, but you lack the requisite power to accomplish the goal on your own. New dangers will arise if you make the attempt

> without help, and since the leader is not strong
> enough to lend assistance, it is a good idea for you
> to extricate yourself completely from the situation.

What was even more surprising to Barry about the reading was its reference to the leader not being strong enough to help him. The chairman of the board was not in good health and was about to retire, and although he was sympathetic to Barry's cause, he was not ready to take on the whole board of directors.

Because line 3 was a moving line, the kua changed into Kua 50, Ting, The Cauldron. The text of Kua 50 reads:

> Ting is the symbol of the cauldron from which spiritual wisdom and information are dispensed. Ting is formed of the trigrams of Li (intelligence and clarity) and Sun (penetrating wind). Together they create penetrating intelligence of a divine nature which is dispensed from the cauldron. This kua brings supreme good fortune and success. By acting with divine wisdom and intelligence, the superior person creates a life of good fortune and success.

Barry liked what the situation turned into, but wasn't sure what he was supposed to do regarding the counsel in line 3. It clearly stated, "extricate yourself completely from the situation." Did that mean he was to resign his position as president? He'd only obtained the presidency two months ago, and he'd worked his whole business life for it. He couldn't just lay it on the line in a power move to force the hand of the board. Or could he? Clearly, he had to do another reading.

His question was, "What will come of my telling the board that if they don't take my recommendation to go into computers that I'll resign?" It gave him a shiver of apprehension just to write the question. The answer was Kua 63, Chi Chi, In Place, In Order. The text reads:

> Perfect order has been accomplished; perfect position and balance have been achieved. Inner and outer harmony prevails. Small accomplishments may be undertaken with success. In the beginning there is good fortune, but it is followed by disorder because it is only when complete order prevails that any misstep brings disorder. It is a law of the Universe that when anything reaches its maximum potential, it turns toward its opposite. The superior person remains aware of the danger and uses relentless care to continue the order and balance as long as possible.

Barry was again amazed at how the reading had first said that his company was in order but out of place, and now was saying that if he forced the hand of the board, his company would be in place and in order. There was a moving line, 4, which reads:

> You have achieved a high position, close to the leader with whom you communicate well. You have the support of your subordinates, and in this time of perfect order, all bodes well. However, danger lurks, and continuous caution is necessary if order is not to degenerate into disorder and your position close to the leader is not to work against you.

By virtue of the moving line, the kua changed into Kua 49, Ko, Achievement. The text of Kua 49 reads:

> When the time for a change is at hand, you will inspire the confidence of those who will assist you in bringing about the change. By ceaselessly following a correct path, you will achieve supreme success, and all occasions for remorse will pass by you. It will benefit you and those around you to organize your schedules and carefully make plans for the coming change.

Barry thought that the reading was almost too good to be true. It was actually telling him how to proceed and saying that he would be successful.

Barry interpreted the reading to mean that he was to lay his presidency on the line with the board. They either had to follow his recommendation or accept his resignation. More than that, it was telling him that if he did that, he'd win and achieve success. He knew that danger was lurking; it always was when one had risen as high as he had, but he'd be cautious.

He called in his most trusted associates in the company and told them of his plan. He knew from his own knowledge of them and from the reading that he had their support, that they thought the way he did, but he wanted to make sure that they were with him. They were.

When the board met, Barry stood in front of them and told them how pleased he was that they had chosen him to lead the company through their next period of growth. Although most of them knew of the path he had followed on his rise to the presidency, he told them the story of his journey from the mail room to the leadership of the company. He told them of the many changes he had gone through, and that the company had gone through, and of the changes the company still had to go through if it were to rise to the top of the industry.

He told of his plan to expand the company into computers. At that, there was a lot of grumbling and uneasiness in the room. The directors didn't want that and he knew it.

He continued. He told them that from what he knew about Universal laws, everything was in motion all the time. A company was either expanding or shrinking. Very seldom, if ever, did a company stay at the same level, and he produced growth charts from the top 100 companies in America to prove it. So sure was he that their company must either go into computers or fall into obscurity in a few years, that he was laying his new presidency on the line. At that, there were gasps of amazement from several members of the board. He'd certainly caught their attention. He told them that there were to be no half-way measures on the issue. If the board was not willing to trust his judgment on the way to run the company, the board would have to find themselves another leader. There was a lot more discussion, and the board tried to talk him out of his ultimatum, but he stuck to his position. He said the most important move he could make for the company was to take it into the computer business. He said that he knew they could not make up their minds on the instant, and so he suggested that they adjourn their meeting for a week, during which time they could call upon him individually or collectively, and, at the end of that time, they could decide.

During the one week period, as Barry had anticipated, the board met with many of his associates. His associates all came back to him and reported that they had supported him one hundred percent.

A week later, the board met and told Barry that he was their choice to lead the company and if it was his decision to go into computers, he could do it and with their blessing. He had won, and he had won big.

Today, Barry is still at the head of his company, but now as chairman of the board of directors.

Sharks

I met Sara and her daughter, Shauna, while I was walking on the beach in Big Sur, California. They were there to participate in a shore dive with a group of other scuba divers. They had arrived early to be able to enjoy the morning on the beach before the others arrived, and Shauna was sitting on the sand reading, *A Tale of The I Ching*. I did not tell her I had written the book, but asked Shauna if she liked what she was reading. She said she did, and asked me if knew anything about the I Ching. I said I did. She asked me if I had ever done an I Ching reading. I told her that I had. She asked how it had come out. I told her that I had done many readings and I was generally very pleased with them. She asked how long I had been using the I Ching. I said for a great many years. She asked me if I used the book regularly. I said that for the first ten or fifteen years I used it regularly, but that, as the years passed, and I came to be more in harmony with the ever-unfolding Universe, and as I became more aware of the laws of the Universe, I used it less and less frequently.

She told me that she and her mother were both long-time users of the I Ching and had even used it once when they had a question about whether or not to dive in waters where sharks had been sighted. Shauna's mother came over at that point and I asked them how it had come about that they were diving where there were sharks. They told me the story that follows. When they had finished telling me the story, Sara asked if I had ever risked my life on the outcome of a reading. I said I had, several times. Shauna asked me if I had ever read any of Wu Wei's books. At that point, I felt that I was bordering on the point of dishonesty not to tell her I had written the book she was holding. I did. They were delighted and excited, and laughed like children. When I told them I was going to write this book, they asked if I would include their story. I told them I would, and that I believed that it would be an inspiration to others who used the I Ching. I hope you find it so.

Sara and Shauna flew to Cozumel, Mexico on the Yucatan Peninsula for a vacation. They were both water enthusiasts and as part of their vacation, had planned a beach dive using scuba gear. Shauna had heard that at night there were lobsters that could be caught and she wanted to catch her own lobster and cook it. Shauna felt it was good to be self-reliant and know about the food chain. She had long ago resolved that if she wasn't willing to catch it and kill it, she wasn't willing to eat it. She told me she didn't want to learn how to hunt in the supermarket.

The third day of their vacation was the time set aside for their first night dive. They had all the necessary equipment, and they hired a guide who was a local divemaster. During breakfast on the day of their dive, they overheard a boat captain talking about sharks. The captain and his crew had seen a number of sharks in the area where Sara and Shauna were going to dive that night. Sharks are nocturnal creatures who hunt at night. The women were cautious and concerned at what they had heard from the captain and the crew, and they asked around to see if the crews of any of the other boats had seen sharks. Sure enough, three other people on different boats had spotted sharks, and all were in the region where the dive was planned. They found their divemaster and asked him what he had heard. He reported that sharks had been sighted in the area of the dive site, and said that if the women wanted to cancel the dive, he would refund their money. The two women were really afraid, but they also really wanted to dive. They had come a long way and didn't want to miss their chance to go lobster hunting. However, neither did they want to become the hunted.

After breakfast, Sara and Shauna, decided to do an I Ching reading. They went back to their room so they would not be disturbed. Sara asked the question. "What will Shauna and I experience diving for lobsters tonight?" The answer was Kua 11, T'ai, Peaceful Prosperity, Harmony, Heaven on Earth. The kua reads:

This kua is formed of the upper trigram of earth, whose motion is downward, and the lower trigram of heaven, whose motion is upward. The two come together, forming the condition of heaven on earth. The light force is in the ascendancy, and the dark force is diminishing. People in high places are considerate of their subordinates, and subordinates are respectful and helpful to those in power. It is a time when feuds end and friendships renew. Harmony prevails; pettiness ends. People act from their higher natures rather than from their lower. There is perfect correspondence in all areas, meaning that everyone gets along with everyone else. It is a time of good fortune and success, a time when small efforts bring large rewards. This time of harmony can be lengthened by healing dissension, making an extra effort to get along with others, being extra courteous and considerate, and participating in every way that is in accord with this time of Heaven on Earth.

Sara and Shauna were happy with the answer. A peaceful dive was just what they wanted. They received a moving line, the bottom line, which reads:

The time of harmony and prosperity is just beginning. You have the necessary strength to begin the

movement toward success and the necessary
charisma to draw other strong people along
with you. To begin a project at this time brings
good fortune.

As a result of the moving line, Kua 11 became Kua 46, Shêng, Advance. The text reads:

To advance at this time brings supreme success. It is
essential that you seek guidance and assistance
from the leader or a highly qualified person. You
need not be fearful; a successful outcome is certain.
By achieving many small goals, you will achieve a
major goal. Being loyal and devoted will benefit you.

Sara and Shauna decided that the prospects were excellent. The text of Kua 46 specifically reads:

You need not be fearful; a successful outcome
is certain.

They would dive. They already had found the expert the reading referred to, their divemaster, and they sought him out again and went over every detail of their dive plans.

As the day passed and the women waited for nightfall to begin their dive, both of them had time to reflect on whether or not they wanted to stake their lives on an I Ching reading. Shauna had only been doing readings for a year, but their accuracy in describing the situations surrounding her questions and the way they "saw through to the heart of things" had convinced her of their infallibility if one interpreted them correctly and asked questions with sincerity and reverence. Sara had been doing readings for fifteen years, and it was she who had gotten Shauna started. Sara had long ago come to rely on the I Ching as a trustworthy guide and was willing to make the dive based on the results of her reading.

The women dove. As they entered the water, Sara said that she was as alert as she had ever been in her life. She reported that as the water closed over her head and she switched on her powerful light, she realized that they were entering a different world; a world where the shark was king and they were just part of his food chain. They dived to about thirty-five feet and swam along the ocean floor, searching in the rocks and crevices for lobsters, but always looking in every direction for sharks.

As they played their lights on the ocean floor, suddenly, from the dark beyond the reach of their lights, Shauna saw several indistinct shapes moving. She nudged her mother and indicted the shapes. Sara added the strength of her light to that of Shauna's and what they saw were three huge sharks about twenty feet in length. They stopped still in the water. The divemaster came to them and waited with them, everyone following the movements of the sharks. The women said that their hearts were beating so loudly they could hear them. Shauna said that she was terribly frightened. Soon, the three sharks were joined by two others. The sharks came closer, their long tails thrashing about. Sara said she wished at that moment that she were anywhere else in the world except under the ocean in Cozumel.

As they were watching, a large lobster came out of a hole in the cliff wall next to them and moved onto the ocean floor. Shauna said that she was so excited by seeing the lobster, she almost went after it. As they watched the lobster walk around, foraging for food, another lobster came out of the same hole, this one larger than the first. It, too, began to search for food. It was at that moment that the sharks disappeared. They whisked away as if something had frightened them. One instant they were there, watching the group, the next instant they were gone. The trio waited a few minutes, but they didn't come back. Sara poked Shauna with her elbow and pointed to the lobsters. With one accord, they went after them.

Sara caught a three-pound lobster, and Shauna, a five-pound lobster. Later that evening, after they had changed and showered, the hotel chef barbecued the lobsters for them, and they drank wine and dined on fresh lobster. They told me of how that night they celebrated the dive, the reading, their courage, and the Universe of which they were a part and to which they could look for unerring guidance. Life, they said, was so much sweeter after being so close to death.

Patience

The young man in this story, Alex, worked part-time in a book store one summer where I gave a one-day seminar on the I Ching, and although he didn't attend the seminar, he overheard bits and pieces of it. After the seminar, he asked if I would show him how to use the yarrow stalks, which I did. Alex's dad died of a heart attack several years before I met him, and he lived at home with his mother who was a registered nurse. He showed his mother how to use the yarrow stalks, and she became very serious about the use of the I Ching. Alex called me occasionally with questions, and on one of those occasions, he asked my advice concerning the following story. I followed his progress as the story unfolded.

Alex wanted a motorcycle. He had his heart set on it. His mother was dead set against it. She was a nurse at the county hospital and had seen too many motorcycle accident victims carried into the hospital on stretchers, their heads smashed, their limbs crushed, their skin torn off, and, in some cases, dead. They agreed that Alex would do an I Ching reading, and whatever it said, they would both abide by it.

Alex's question was: "What can I expect if I buy a motorcycle at this time?" The answer was Kua 51, Chên, Shock, The Arousing.

The kua reads:

Shock! A manifestation of God. It usually causes fear and trembling, but the superior person does not let the shock drive from his mind the awareness that he is a divine creature in a divine Universe and that the shock was entirely for his benefit. He retains his reverence for All-That-Is. Such reverence brings success. After sustaining a shock, the superior person examines his life to see whether he is a good person and accomplishing good things. He then orders his life according to the highest principles.

The last thing Alex wanted to get was a shock of the kind the Universe can deliver. However, the kua said that the shock would be for his benefit. Perhaps he should risk it. His mother didn't think he would like the lesson.

There was a moving line, the top line. The text of the top line reads:

The shock has reached terrifying proportions, and everyone is numbly staring, unable to take action.

To try to advance at this time brings misfortune. If
you have not been affected by the shock, but your
friends or associates have, no blame will attach to
you, but afterward they will talk about you.

Alex's mother was certain that it was going to be she who
was numbly staring at Alex as his body was wheeled into the
hospital. Alex had to agree that his mother was most likely
correct about the reading.

The kua into which Kua 51 turned by virtue of the top
moving line was Kua 21, Shih Ho, Corrective Punishment.
The text of Kua 21 reads:

This kua depicts being punished and punishing
others, primarily, but not solely, for criminal
offenses. It is favorable to administer justice, which
brings success. The best way to deter wrongdoers
is to make the law absolutely clear and to make
punishment swift and certain.

Alex had come to believe that if he bought his motorcycle at that time he would have a serious accident. The idea
of buying a motorcycle was wisely put on the shelf.

A year later, Alex did another reading asking the same
question. That time the response was different. The answer
was Kua 29, K'an, Danger, the Abyss. The kua reads:

The danger that now threatens is objective danger, meaning that the danger stems from an outside source. In most situations, the danger can be overcome by correct action. When danger cannot be overcome, you must simply endure it. Danger has its important use in sharpening the mind and causing us to prepare for adversity. Those who are well-informed should instruct others. Remaining virtuous and persevering is the best course of action when confronted by danger.

There were no moving lines.

As long as there was danger in the reading, Alex was not going to buy a motorcycle. He waited another year and then asked the same question again. This time his answer was Kua 54, Kuei Mei, Joyous Movement. The kua says:

The ancient text uses the symbolism of a maiden in the various stages of being taken into a Chinese household: first as a concubine, then as a slave, then as a wife, and then as a daughter given in marriage. This symbolism is no longer appropriate, but we have the original meaning of the trigrams to guide us, along with the meaning of the individual lines. The primary characteristic of the lower trigram is joy, and the primary characteristic of the upper trigram is arousing movement. Therefore, joyous movement. If you are entering into a relationship or group, use great care and give respect to those with whom you must integrate. Because the four lines of the inner structure of the kua are not in their correct positions, that is, the strong lines are in weak positions and the weak lines are in strong positions, and because all but two of the six lines show improper correspondence with each other, the pronouncement of the kua is misfortune. Nothing should be undertaken. If you must undertake something, do it joyfully and use extreme caution.

Alex had mixed feelings about the meaning of the kua. Joyous movement sounded all right, but misfortune did not. However, the kua said that if he had to undertake something—like the purchase of his motorcycle, he should do it joyfully and use extreme caution. There was a moving line, the bottom line. The text of the bottom line reads:

You have the necessary strength to move joyously forward, but you are only at the beginning of the situation, and you do not have the support of those in power. There is also a person just above you who will try to block any attempt you make to advance.

> Your best course of action at this moment is to bide
> your time and wait for a more favorable situation
> to develop.

That was something he could clearly understand. The person in power whose support he did not have and who would block his attempt to get his motorcycle was his mother. The moving line said he was to bide his time and wait for a more favorable situation to develop. He waited.

Six months passed, and his mother became ill. She was out of work and needed Alex to help bring in some money. He would have to drop out of college for a year and find work. Alex knew of a messenger company in town who would hire messengers if they had motorcycles. Two of his friends had motorcycles and maybe they could all get jobs with the same company. It was a well-paying job, and the messenger company would buy liability insurance for them. Alex talked it over with his mother, who was still opposed to it, but she said that he should do a reading and she would abide by the guidance provided in the reading. Alex did the reading. His question was: "What can I expect as a result of buying a motorcycle at this time?" The answer was again Kua 54, Kuei Mei, Joyous movement, but this time there were two moving lines, 2 and 5. Alex told me he laughed when he read the lines, they were so accurate in depicting the situation at home. Line 2 reads:

You are well positioned and have the necessary strength to move forward joyously. You also have the support of the leader, who is weak and, therefore, looks to you for support. You will be able to advance now without hindrance. Good fortune.

Line 5 reads:

You are in the leadership position and would like to move joyously and vigorously forward to carry out your aims to benefit the people. You have the help and support of a very strong and well positioned subordinate and also the help and support of your strong right hand person. [Alex's mother and two friends] There is no one to hinder you, and because this is the time of vigorous, joyous movement, you may move forward with confidence. Good fortune.

The moving line caused the kua to change into Kua 17, Leading and Following. Kua 17 reads:

Joyous movement attracts followers. By following the path of the superior person, persevering in what is good and right, fair and just, you will be greatly benefited, and no blame will attach to your progress. Modesty is essential at this time. Because

of the rigorous activity required in this time of leading or following, the superior person takes time for
rest and recuperation. He makes a time to be still
and nourishes himself properly. This kua indicates
supreme success.

That was the reading Alex had been waiting for. It was a
clear indication that he could move safely forward. His
mother was in complete agreement, but still fearful for Alex's
safety. She said that even though she believed in the reading,
she had seen so many motorcycle accidents, she couldn't help
feeling apprehensive. Alex bought his motorcycle, got jobs
for himself and his two friends, took good care of himself,
made sure he ate properly, rested enough, and at the end
of his first year as a messenger, he was put in charge of twelve
other messengers. He didn't need his motorcycle any longer,
so he sold it and bought a small car. He went back to school
and finished in three years with a degree in computer sci-
ences. Alex's mother died a few weeks after he obtained his
degree. He told me that at her funeral he read from wu wei's
book, *I Ching Wisdom*. The saying he read was the second
one in the book. It reads:

> *To a person of true understanding*
> *it makes no difference*
> *whether death comes early or late.*

Wu Wei's comment:

He cultivates himself and uses his time productively. His sense of the transitoriness of life does not impel him to uninhibited revelry in order to enjoy life while it lasts, nor to yield to melancholy and sadness, thereby spoiling the time remaining to him. Secure in the knowledge that all is one, he experiences himself as much a part of the Universe as the stars and the trees; as enduring as All-That-Is. Knowing that time is only an illusion, he feels no break with time. Understanding this, you need have no fear of the moment of death, which is only a point of transition, such as walking through a doorway from one room into another and no more remarkable than any other moment.

The Empire State Building

Ten years ago a friend, Cheryl, came to me for advice. She was a few months pregnant and her boyfriend, David, wouldn't marry her. They were both exceptionally fine people, but the young man was afraid of responsibility and was threatening to move to another state.

I invited Cheryl and David to my home for dinner the following week along with several other friends. After dinner we were sitting around the fire talking and one of the dinner guests asked me a questions about the I Ching. I told them the history of the I Ching and explained the theory behind the process of divination. David didn't know anything about the I Ching and was very skeptical of the whole idea of divination. He said that the notion that one could ask questions and have them answered by the Universe with absolute accuracy was preposterous. I suggested that he ask a question and use the yarrow stalks to find the answer. I told him that one should not approach the I Ching with an air of frivolity, but with reverence and sincerity. He laughed and said he didn't think he could muster up much reverence, but that he'd do it for the fun of it.

I asked him if he would like to go with me to another room where he could do his reading in private, but he said that it would be more fun to do it where everyone could hear his question and the answer he received. I said that he should ask the question that was uppermost in his mind. Everyone in the room knew of his situation with Cheryl, and we all knew what David's question should be, namely, "What is the best course of action for me to take with regard to Cheryl?"

I provided David with a piece of paper and a pen and told him how to proceed. David refused to take the situation seriously and chose for his question, "Will the Empire State Building in New York City fall down next year?" I asked him if there was not a question that was more important to him than that one, but he laughed and said no. I suggested that David re-phrase his question so that it would not require a yes or no answer, but he refused.

I said that I would not participate in such a silly question. He asked me if I was afraid of the answer making the I Ching look silly. I said that I was not afraid for the I Ching, but that I believed that frivolous questions should not be asked, and I would not therefore participate.

Another of the dinner guests who was a long-time friend of mine and who I had taught to use the yarrow stalks years ago, volunteered to guide David through the process. They used the Wilhelm/Baynes translation of the I Ching, and

David's answer was Kua 31, Hsien, Attraction, Influence. There were no moving lines. The kua spoke of "courtship and marriage, the foundations of all social relationships." The judgment reads:

> **Influence. Success. Perseverance furthers. To take a maiden to wife brings good fortune.**

David was reading the answer aloud and when his friends heard the reading, they began to laugh. David laughed too, but his face flushed red with embarrassment, and he became very nervous. They said they were not laughing at David, but at the way he had been provided with a perfect answer to the question he should have asked.

David suddenly became very serious and thoughtful. He excused himself and asked Cheryl to walk with him in the garden. When they returned fifteen or twenty minutes later, it was to announce that they were going to be married immediately. Everyone cheered and applauded. David was very happy, and, having made the decision, knew it was the right one.

That was ten years ago, and now, at the time of this writing, David and Cheryl have three lovely children, two boys and a girl. Their marriage has turned out to be wonderful for them both. I am also happy to report that David is now a good student of the I Ching.

Prostate Cancer

Richard developed prostate cancer when he was fifty-nine years old. The prostate is a walnut-sized gland in a man's pelvic area just below the bladder that produces seminal fluid. Richard had gone to see his family doctor for a routine checkup that included a blood test, and discovered he had an elevated PSA score. PSA stands for prostate specific antigen. The antigen, which continually leaks itself into the bloodstream, leaks an elevated amount whenever a man's prostate gets into trouble. The trouble doesn't have to be from cancer, but can be from a variety of different problems. The prostate is the only gland that produces that specific antigen and it only produces elevated amounts of it when the prostate gets into some kind of difficulty. Usually a healthy prostate produces a PSA score of about two or three. If the score gets over five, there is a strong indication that the prostate gland is at the beginning of a problem.

When Richard had his checkup, his PSA score was sixteen, which is a highly elevated score. The doctor recommended that Richard see an oncologist, a physician who treats cancerous tumors. The oncologist ordered a biopsy of

Richard's prostate, and the results revealed that he had prostate cancer on the right lobe of his prostate. The biopsy also revealed that the cancer was aggressive, meaning that it was fast growing.

Richard did an I Ching reading asking what action he should take regarding his prostate cancer. The answer was Kua 18, Correcting Deficiencies. Kua 18 reads:

> At this time, there is a great opportunity to take a major step forward. There is a deficiency in your situation that will be greatly to your advantage to correct. The deficiency may be psychological, having to do with beliefs you are holding that are not in accord with the truth of the situation, or it may be that some aspect of your external life requires improvement. The deficiency may include your physical health, your work, your love relationship, your business relationships and related business matters, your spiritual well-being, financial matters, or undertakings of any nature. The deficiencies most likely exist in the situation surrounding your question.
>
> Regarding psychological deficiencies, throughout your life until now, you have been taught lessons. Some of those lessons may not have been in accord with Universal law or truth. By acting in accord with those lessons, you may have brought misfortune your

way. You may also have adopted behavior patterns
that are not only not benefiting you, but are creating
problems for you. When you begin correcting psycho-
logical conditions, asking those who know you well to
sincerely tell you what improvements they think you
could make will be of great benefit to you. Be open-
minded about their suggestions, even though you
may feel hurt or offended by what they say.

Clinging to past hurts and injuries is foolish, and
is one of the most important inner conditions you
can change. What happened is finished, even if it
happened only yesterday. We cannot change past
events, but we can change how we view them. If
you are permitting events from your past to bring
you pain today, you are the foolish one who is giving those events their power to hurt you. Whatever
the event was, whether it hurt you, took something
from you, betrayed you, violated you, or caused you
mental or physical pain, it is over. It has no power
to hurt you beyond that which you give it—and
what you give, you can take away. Because you live
in a Universe where everything that happens benefits you, continuing to carry hurts from the past
shows that you lack true understanding of your Universe, and alerts you to an important deficiency that
you can begin correcting immediately.

The feelings you hold in your mind manifest in your body. It is the nature of the mind to create, and what you hold there will somehow manifest itself in your body. If you hold worry and anxiety in your mind, they will appear in your body as pain, disease, stress, and illness. If you hold gratitude, joy, and reverence in your mind, they will manifest as glowing, radiant health. That you are consulting the I Ching at this time shows that you have already begun learning lessons that are in accord with Universal truth.

If you have a shortcoming that is obvious to you, or if there is an obvious deficiency in your situation, it is serious indeed and requires immediate attention. You must plan carefully if you are to reach your goal. Once you begin taking corrective measures, keep a careful eye on your progress so that regression does not set in. Through constant perseverance in healing the deficiency inherent within yourself or the situation, you will eventually reach your goal.

As the ancient text states, "Before the starting point, three days; after the starting point, three days." This refers to the time you need to spend defining what you need to change, planning the changes, and continuing to be watchful as your plan

**unfolds. By being diligent in your efforts, and perse-
vering until you reach your goal, you will enjoy
supreme success and great good fortune.**

There were no moving lines. Richard interpreted the
reading to mean that he should seek to cure his deficiency
rather than have his prostate removed surgically, even though
the oncologist recommended it. Richard immediately started
to research holistic medicine cures. He pursued several holistic healing remedies and followed them religiously. Three
months later he again had his PSA score checked and found
that his score had elevated to twenty. His doctor urged him
to have his prostate removed immediately so the cancer
would not spread to other parts of his body. Richard was
frightened by the elevated PSA score and did a reading to
see what he could expect if he had his prostate removed surgically. The answer was Kua 19: Advancing, Progress.

**This is a fortunate time when your advances will be
crowned with supreme success. You must make the
best use of this time of rapid, easy advance by acting
with great determination and perseverance, for it will
not last forever. The ancient text states that you
should be untiring in your leadership and teaching
and unlimited in your patience, tolerance, and pro-
tection of people. To be tolerant, means to overlook**

others' faults and mistakes. Overlook even intentional transgressions, for that will prevent arguments and ensure your continued success. During this time of rapid advance, be tireless in bringing your plans to completion. This is the time for action. Do not be fearful, for your success is certain. If you see a problem coming, you can neutralize it before it grows strong. However, if the setback does occur, do not be dismayed. In the end, it will work to your complete benefit, particularly if you act as if the only reason it has occurred was so that you could benefit.

The moving line was number two:

You are strong and have advanced to a key position. By finding someone with whom you can join forces or by joining a group, you will make greater advances than you can alone. Joining and advancing will bring you good fortune, and everything that occurs will benefit you. By acting in accord with all that is highest and best within yourself, you will see your plans come to fruition. If you act honorably and according to the principles of the superior person, you will travel the paths of life swiftly, honestly, and courageously, and you will find good fortune.

The result was Kua 24, Return of the Light Force.

The forces of light and dark, which represent good and evil, alternate constantly. An increase of one always leads to a decrease of the other. This kua indicates that the time of darkness is past, bringing the victory of the light that is now in the ascendancy. This is a time for you to look inward, to be in touch with the Divine within you, and to perceive your inner light, which is the ascending force of life in nature and in you. To sense that inner light is to experience your oneness with All-That-Is. The return of the light force brings great good fortune. Projects are blessed, relationships prosper, feuds end, friendships are reborn, and people are kinder and more thoughtful to each other. It is a time when people act from their higher natures rather than their lower. It is a time of rejoicing because the return of the light force brings with it the blessings of the Universe. You can magnify the influence of this time by striving to be the best person you can be. This kua indicates that success is forthcoming, that friends will come to your aid, and that having somewhere to go or something to do will enhance your position. Even superior persons, no matter how careful they are, sometimes stray from the path of light, which is the path of abundant life. It is crucial that you realize when you have strayed from that path and that you turn back before going too far because otherwise you will "fall into the pit," meaning that you will suffer misfortune.

Having received this kua, reflect on your character and your actions, as well as the results that you have achieved, to see if you have strayed from the right path that will bring you the best and greatest benefits. If your life is not unfolding as you wish, it can only be because you have strayed from the path of light and need to make basic inner changes. If you do, you will find your way back to the right path, where you will again find great good fortune.

Because the light force is just returning, be gentle with yourself and avoid trying to accomplish too much too soon. To begin a small undertaking will meet with success. The return of the light force is a powerful time indeed, for all the beneficial forces of the Universe will now be exerting their influences in your behalf.

Acting on the basis of the reading, Richard scheduled an appointment to have his prostate removed. The operation was successful, and two months later, Richard's PSA score was zero. He was completely without prostate cancer.

Several years passed and Richard had another physical checkup. He went to an alternative medicine doctor who said Richard's testosterone and DHEA levels were low and suggested he start a regimen of testosterone and DHEA. DHEA stands for dehydroepiandrosterone, which is a natural, intermediate steroid hormone produced in our body by the adrenal glands. DHEA is a precursor to testosterone, and testosterone is suspected to play a part in the onset of prostate cancer.

Richard decided that he would do an I Ching reading before he took either of those supplements. Following the instructions in his *I Ching Workbook*, he described his situation and then asked, "What can I expect if I take testosterone and DHEA supplements?" The answer was Kua 52, Kên that means, Mountain—Stopping—Thoughts Coming to Rest. The first paragraph of the kua gives the answer without room for doubt:

Universal law provides that every condition has a time for advancing or movement and a time for stopping or rest, and that each comes at its proper time. This is the time for stopping; so, with regard to your question, stop, and take no further action at this time. To do otherwise will lead to misfortune. There are times when the best action is no action, and this is one of those times."

There were no moving lines.

Richard wisely did not follow the doctor's advice about taking testosterone and DHEA. A few weeks later, he called his oncologist and asked him what he thought about taking testosterone and DHEA. The oncologist said, "Under no circumstances should you take those supplements because if there are any remaining cancer cells, they could be reactivated."

Richard said that without having the benefit of the reading, he may have followed the first doctor's advice and taken the supplements.

Modesty, Modesty, and More Modesty

A few months before I began writing this book, I received an e-mail from the man in this story. He had a question about one of his readings. We communicated back and forth on the internet for a few weeks during which time I told him I was going to write this book. He called me on the telephone and told me the following story for inclusion in the book.

Ralph, an author who lives in California, wrote a self help book about being able to live life the way you want to. He found an agent in New York, Bernice, to represent him, and the agent submitted the book to editors at various major publishing houses. After a month, Bernice received a letter of interest from an editor at a major New York publishing house that has earned a fine reputation. The letter said that the work was being submitted to other company editors for their approval and that the editor would contact Bernice when the process was finished.

Bernice and Ralph were elated. After several more weeks of waiting, the editor called Bernice and said the other editors liked the book, but it now had to be submitted to the president. Two more weeks went by. The editor again called Bernice and said the president liked the book but believed that since the author would be appearing on radio and TV to promote the book, that the success of the book depended on the author, and asked if he would fly to New York for an interview.

Ralph was excited. He did an I Ching reading asking, "What can I do to have the best interview with the president of the publishing house?" He received as an answer Kua 15, Ch'ien, Modesty.

The text reads:

Modesty creates success. The Superior man carries things through.

Ralph, a sometimes egotistical, and always enthusiastic person, vowed to himself that he would remain modest no matter what came his way. The moving line was Line 2.

Out of the fullness of the heart the mouth speaketh.

The guidance of line two could not have been more clear. Because of the moving line, Kua 15 became Kua 46, Shêng, Advance:

Pushing upward has supreme success. One must
see the great man. Fear not.

Ralph was elated. He believed he could not miss getting
his book published. He bought a new suit and, full of confidence, saying over and over to himself, "modesty and adapt-
ability," flew to New York. On the day of the interview, he and
Bernice went to the publisher's building where they were
shown into a large conference room. In a few minutes six
women came in, each representing a different area of expertise of the corporate staff: promotion, distribution, design and
layout, etc. Soon, Mr. Graves, the president of the publishing house came into the room and introduced himself. Everyone sat around a large table, each of the women taking turns
firing questions at Ralph to test the extent of his knowledge.
Ralph held up well until the president took his turn. He asked
Ralph a sensitive question regarding the major theme of his
book, namely, that a person can be what he wants and have
what he wants. Ralph responded enthusiastically.

Mr. Graves began asking ever more pointed questions
to which Ralph gave ever more heated answers. Before long,
they were in a full-fledged argument, Ralph defending brilliantly the position stated in his book. When the argument
was over he had clearly won. Mr. Graves had been van-
quished. He excused himself from the meeting and left.

The six women were obviously impressed with Ralph, and as the meeting broke up, they all congratulated him on his success.

Back at his hotel room, Ralph was feeling greatly exhilarated over his interview and got out his I Ching and his yarrow stalks and did a reading to find out just how great a success he had achieved. His question was, "How did I make out with the publisher?" The answer was Kua 36, Ming I, Persecution.

A man of dark nature in a position of authority brings harm to the wise and able man.

Ralph realized he had made an error. He had failed to remain modest and had instead become aggressive and immodest. He believed the publisher would retaliate. By virtue of the moving line, Kua 36 became Kua 15, Modesty, Humbleness, Moderation. It was an extra slap on the wrist. Ralph packed his bags and went home. A week later Bernice called Ralph and told him that she had received a letter from the publisher saying they would not buy Ralph's book.

Earthquake!

The girl in this story heard a radio program in which I was being interviewed about the I Ching. After the program was over, she called me and asked several questions about statements in the I Ching on which she was not clear. She also told me the details of the following story which I have included for your consideration. Jenny was thoughtful enough to send me copies of her readings.

Jenny moved from Denver, Colorado to Los Angeles, California in 1980. There she learned of the San Andreas fault, a crack in the earth's crust that runs from Oregon to Mexico. The fault was caused by two giant tectonic plates, one that basically supports the Pacific Ocean and the other that basically supports North America, moving in divergent directions. Jenny did some research and learned that many seismologists were predicting a massive earthquake to occur at some point in time, they didn't know exactly when, which would have the potential to destroy one or more of several cities, among them, Los Angeles. They couldn't, however, predict the time.

Jenny told me that for some reason unknown to her, she was not uncomfortable knowing she lived in an earthquake zone, and settled down to enjoy life in her new home. A few years later she saw a program on television that told of an unusual time in cosmic history that was going to take place in a few months. It was a time when all nine planets of our solar system would be lined up, one behind the other. That particular cosmic event only takes place every several hundred years. Some seismologists were predicting that the pull on the earth, caused by the increased gravity of the planets being in line, would exert enough influence on the giant tectonic plates to trigger a huge quake at the San Andreas fault line.

All of Jenny's alarm bells went off. Maybe she should visit her parents in Colorado until the line up of the planets had passed; maybe it was time take a long desired vacation to Europe. She decided to ask. Jenny had used the I Ching for about five years and had come to trust the information she received in the readings. She got out her yarrow stalks and did a reading. Her statement and question were: "There are some predictions for an earthquake to occur in the Los Angeles area when the nine planets line up. What action should I take with regard to my safety." The answer was Kua 5 Hsü, Holding Back in the Face of Danger. The text of Kua 5 reads:

> This kua depicts a strong person below, who
> desires to advance, and grave danger above, which

threatens the one who advances. To wait until the danger passes is the correct action, for to advance in the face of this great danger would be foolhardy. However, because the lower trigram is composed of three strong lines, the people or groups of people they represent will ultimately be successful in their advance, provided that they remain true to their natures, which are light-giving, pure, and virtuous. It will be of benefit to begin a major undertaking or journey when the time of waiting is past, whichever is called for. During the time of waiting, the superior person clarifies his plans, feasts, maintains a joyous and promising outlook, and is unconcerned, knowing he will ultimately reach his goal.

Jenny looked at what the reading counseled and took from it the following statements: "grave danger above, which threatens the one who advances." Jenny thought that meant that if she advanced, meaning that she would leave the area, she might encounter danger from a source other than the earthquake, or that if she left the area, she might suffer some misfortune by missing some opportunity that she could have taken advantage of had she remained at home. "To wait until the danger passes is the correct action." That was clear enough to her way of thinking. It meant, "Stay home." "It will be of benefit to begin a major undertaking or journey when the time of waiting is past." Again, she believed that meant, "Stay home."

Line 5 was a moving line. The text of Line 5 reads:

> **You are strong and in a place of leadership. Even though you are surrounded by danger, you are confident of your own strength and resources and, therefore, are comfortable enough to enjoy dining. To persevere in a righteous path and to remain confident brings good fortune.**

Jenny wasn't so sure that she was confident of her own strength and resources, but the reading said she should persevere in a righteous path and remain confident. She also interpreted "to enjoy dining," as an indication that she was to remain home and enjoy dining, another way of saying, "relax." Kua 5, by virtue of its moving line, became Kua 11, Ta'i, Peaceful Prosperity, Harmony, Heaven on Earth. The text of Kua 11 reads:

> **This kua is formed of the upper trigram of Earth, whose motion is downward, and the lower trigram of Heaven, whose motion is upward. The two come together, forming the condition of heaven on earth. The light force is in the ascendancy, and the dark force is diminishing. People in high places are con-**

siderate of their subordinates, and subordinates are respectful and helpful to those in power. It is a time when feuds end and friendships renew. Harmony prevails; pettiness ends. People act from their higher natures rather than from their lower. There is perfect correspondence in all areas, meaning that everyone gets along with everyone else. It is a time of good fortune and success, a time when small efforts bring large rewards. This time of harmony can be lengthened by healing dissension, making an extra effort to get along with others, being extra courteous and considerate, and participating in every way that is in accord with this time of Heaven on Earth.

That settled matters in Jenny's mind. There was nothing in Line 5 that said that the situation would turn out to be anything other than peaceful. She stayed in Los Angeles. The time of the line up of the planets came and went and no unusual earthquake activity occurred. Not only that, she had a particularly peaceful and happy time.

Increase and Decrease

The following story happened two years ago. I was on the island of Oahu when Mr. Alberts came there to begin his project. One of the real estate brokers involved in the land development project is a good friend of mine and he introduced me to Mr. Alberts. When Mr. Alberts found out that I was interested in the I Ching, he told me he was on the island as result of a reading he had done two weeks previous. He kept me aware of his progress through the transaction, and later gave me his permission to use his story in this book.

Mr. Alberts, a negotiator who lived in Denver, Colorado, was asked by Mr. Roberts, a Hawaiian businessman, to undertake a difficult and lengthy negotiation on the island of Oahu to recover a great deal of money that was owed to Mr. Roberts by the men who were his partners in a land development deal. He said his partners had been dishonest with him, which caused him to sustain heavy money losses and to be in poor financial condition. Mr. Roberts said that he did not even have enough money to pay Mr. Alberts for his work, but that if Mr. Alberts was successful in recovering Mr. Roberts' money, he would pay him his normal fee plus a large bonus from the money recovered.

Mr. Alberts was concerned that he might do a great amount of work and receive no financial remuneration for his efforts if he was not able to recover the money for Mr. Roberts. He made an I Ching inquiry. His question was, "What financial outcome can I expect as a result of undertaking the negotiation on Oahu for Mr. Roberts?" He received as an answer Kua 41, Sun, Decrease. "Well," he thought to himself, "that doesn't sound so good for me." The text of Kua 41 reads:

Time inevitably brings increase and decrease. The duration of each can be lengthened or shortened, or their depth can be made greater or lesser, but they cannot be avoided. Increase and decrease in themselves do not presage good or bad times, for either can bring both. What matters is that you recognize the time of each and act accordingly, that you know that one inevitably follows the other, and that you are prepared. In a time of decrease, maintaining your sincerity and a positive attitude will bring about supreme good fortune without any blame attaching to your actions. In this time of decrease, if you find yourself in need

or in scanty circumstances, it would not benefit
you to make a show of wealth simply to impress
others; instead, be modest and thrifty. If a gift
must be given, it is the sincerity of the giver and
the intent with which it is given, rather than the
gift itself, that is important. In this time of
decrease, you will be benefited if you undertake
a project and persevere in your good and virtuous
conduct, remembering that the superior person
controls his anger and does not squander his life
force in debauchery and dissipation.

After giving consideration to the text of the reading,
he concluded that it didn't sound so bad, and the reading
said he would be benefited if he undertook a project. Line 5
was a moving line which reads:

In this time of decrease, you will be greatly
increased. Your increase is decreed from on high,
and none can oppose it. Supreme good fortune.

That put a big smile on the face of Mr. Roberts. He
thought to himself, "The reading is perfect. It recognizes that
Mr. Alberts is in poor financial circumstances, that he is in
a time of decrease, but that even in the midst of his time of
decrease, I will be greatly increased."

He agreed to the terms of his hiring and began the negotiations. He worked for one year, during which time he received no compensation for his services, but at the end of that time the negotiations were successfully concluded and he received his compensation.

As we can see from the above example, the moving line takes precedence over the kua, determining its specific meaning. The kua is of decrease, but the line is for increase. The line takes precedence.

The kua which resulted from the changing of Line 5, was Kua 61, Chung Fu, Emptiness, Openness. The kua reads:

Two broken lines within four unbroken lines depict emptiness. When you can maintain emptiness by not holding prejudiced thoughts, forgone conclusions, or conscious purpose, you will then be open to receiving wisdom and knowledge from other sources: people, objects, the Universe itself. Having received that knowledge and wisdom, you will speak words of such great wisdom that you will be able to influence not only all people but also, as the ancient text reads, the pigs and fishes. Good fortune will inure to your benefit when you practice the pursuit of emptiness. It will benefit you to undertake a major project. Because of the inner clarity that develops within you, you will be able to

discuss difficult problems and resolve them, and
people will do well to wait until you have deliber-
ated on a matter before carrying out their plans.

When Mr. Alberts went to Oahu, he made certain he did
not hold any prejudicial thoughts or preconceived ideas. He
did his best to remain open, and by so doing, received all the
information and wisdom he needed. He reported to me that
everyone was respectful of him and listened to his counsel,
and that he was therefore able to carry out his negotiations
with complete success.

More Earthquakes

Winston, who also lives in California and took one of my workshops reports that he, too, was concerned about the predictions for another earthquake that was to occur on May 6 or 7 in 1993. He did a reading and received as an answer Kua 52, Kên, Mountain, Stopping, Thoughts Coming to Rest. There were no moving lines. The text of Kua 52 reads:

> Universal law provides for the alternation of movement and rest, each at its proper time. If you remain still when the time for action is at hand, you will miss your opportunity, and what would have been easy becomes difficult. If you are in action when the time for rest is at hand, you will be unprepared when the time for action comes. When actions stop and thoughts come to rest, the sanest person achieves a quiet heart.

Winston knew from studying the attributes of each of the trigrams, that the main attribute of Kua 52, which is composed of the doubling of the trigram Ken, was that of stopping or remaining quiet and unmoving. He saw the mountain as broad, solid, immovable, and he interpreted the reading to mean that he was to remain quietly at home. He did, and enjoyed a peaceful time, free from earthquakes.

Walking Your Path

Roger is a publisher. At the stable where he rides horses, he was introduced to a businessman, Charles, whose partner, Sherry, was a writer. She had only written one book, and it was a children's story. They were talking to major publishers in New York, and two were interested. There were also two film producers who were interested in making a movie of the story. They thought it was a story that had the potential of the *Harry Potter* books.

Roger's company was small. He only published three or four books a year, but he was good at what he did and he promoted his books heavily. The writers whose work he published thought the world of him. He was fair with them and always kept his word.

Charles was very impressed with Roger and knew he could get a better deal from Roger than he could from the major publishers, if Roger could actually get Sherry's book into the bookstores and create enough publicity to attract readers. Roger said he could do that, and Charles believed him. Charles said that he would leave the decision up to

Sherry. If she agreed, then it was a deal. The meeting was set for the following week at Spago's, a restaurant in Beverly Hills, California.

Roger asked around and found that Sherry was very temperamental, easy to anger, and extremely sensitive. It was said she would take offense at the slightest cause. He got out his *I Ching Workbook* and did a reading. Following the directions, he first wrote out the situation, describing the proposal and what he knew of Sherry, and then asked, "What do I need to know about Sherry?" The answer was Kua 10, Walking Your Path. There were no moving lines. Roger laughed when he read the text of the kua. It described the situation so perfectly. The text follows:

This kua depicts you "treading on the tail of a tiger," meaning a powerful person or group who can cause you harm. However, even though you tread on the tiger's tail, it will not bite you because you are sincere and agreeable and know how to behave properly.

Such behavior brings you success. The key to your success lies in cultivating a pleasing and sincere personality, which will bring you success and good fortune because the person or group represented by the tiger will trust and respect you. Pleasant manners win over even bad-tempered people. If you do not let their unpleasantness irritate or upset you, your own pleasant manners will have a positive and calming effect on them. Receiving this kua as your answer foretells that you will have success if you accept the guidance of this kua.

At the luncheon, Roger made certain he was agreeable and pleasing. His proposal was very fair, as it was for his other writers. There were several moments during the luncheon when Sherry made a remark that would have ordinarily caused Roger to react aggressively, but he kept his pleasing personality at the forefront. One of Sherry's remarks was, "I've heard a lot about you publishers, how you're out to get what you can from us first time writers; how you take advantage of us at every opportunity." Roger bristled inwardly, but calmly replied, "Oh, have you heard that? I've heard that too, but if you talk to the writers whose work I publish, and I invite you to do that, they will tell you that I'm cut from a different bolt of cloth." Sherry laughed and replied, "You're not easy to provoke, are you?" Roger joined in the laughter and said, " Well, what you said is true, I've heard the same thing from some of my writers who have been published by other companies, but I'm not like that so I take no offense." Later in the conversation, Sherry said, "I heard from my partner that you use the I Ching; I use it too. Did you do a reading about this meeting?" Charles laughed again and said he had, and told her what the reading said. She nodded her head and remarked that she understood why he had been so agreeable. Roger replied that he had heard that she was easy to provoke and could be a tigress when her anger was aroused, he was therefore being extra careful. She replied that it was true, that she was easy to provoke, but found him easy to deal with.

Charles then took a chance and decided to push what he felt was his advantage. He said, "The only way I will publish your book is if you give me the right to publish your next book on the same terms as this first book. Sherry surprised him by agreeing at once.

Charles asked if Sherry had done a reading. Sherry laughed and said she had. She said her question was, "What can I expect if I my book is published by Roger?" Her answer was Kua 45 with no moving lines.

This is a time when you can either join a group or gather others into a group. If you are joining a group, you should have a clear understanding of why you are joining and what you hope to accomplish. The group will have its own goals and reasons for its existence, but you must be clear about your own personal goal or what you want to obtain for yourself by joining. If you are creating a group, you must have a well-defined cause that will draw all the members together and earn their support. To attract followers, you must be enthusiastic about your goal, so that you will gain their interest and ignite their own enthusiasm. The goal must be meaningful and worthwhile, or your members will soon drop out.

Being the leader of a group requires sincerity, strength, and dedication to the group's well-being. Your motives for creating a group must be ethical, moral, and rooted in an inner desire not just to meet your own needs but to be of service to the members and to those outside the group. There is some indication that you can gain valuable information about your undertaking by seeking advice from a qualified person before you begin. Once you define your goal and develop clear-cut guidelines for achieving it, you must always move in the direction of your goal. Your followers will rely on you to set an example, so you will have to show them that you are tireless, dedicated, enthusiastic, and loyal.

Whether you are joining or creating a group, choose your associates with great care. Universal forces are at work bringing together those who belong together. At this time, the Universal forces may bring people to you who may not be to your personal liking but who nonetheless will be of great benefit to you or to the group. According to the ancient text, you should remain open-minded when you are either talking with members of a group you are considering joining or talking with potential members of the group you are forming. You need not concern yourself about finding the right people, for they will come. The ancient text also states that you can obtain good fortune by making a great offering. The ancient text urges you to prepare for the unexpected and to take whatever precautions you can to ward off any dangers that might arise. You will be called upon to make sacrifices to obtain your goal. Making sacrifices is appropriate. Success will be yours.

Sherry said that the reading had said she would be called upon to "make a great offering," and she regarded her granting to Roger the right to publish her second book was that offering.

The meeting was exceptional for them both and each felt well supported and well advised by their readings.

The Center

I was in a bookstore purchasing some incense when a man purchased one of my books. He commented to the woman at the cash register that he had purchased all of my other books. She looked at me, knowing who I was, and it was plain that she was silently asking permission to introduce me. I nodded. She introduced me to the man who asked if I would join him for tea. I sat with him for a very pleasant hour during which time he revealed the following story to me.

Timothy belonged to a spiritual group that held meetings every week and broadcast a radio program twice a week. The group had achieved a strong following and was continually advocating that its members solicit other people to join the group. The leaders constantly urged the members to support the group with monetary donations. Although Timothy believed in the message the group was advocating, he felt that the methods were inappropriate for a spiritual group. He also thought that the beliefs were too self-serving, too focused on getting more members and getting more money from the members rather than on helping others. The leader of the group had been urging Timothy to bring in new members and had on many occasions expressed his displeasure with Timothy for not bringing even one new member in the six months since he had first joined the group.

One evening, the leader had a talk with Timothy and told him that if he didn't bring in at least one new member within the next month, he would be asked to leave the group. Timothy became angry and told the leader that his ultimatum to him summed up exactly what Timothy thought was wrong with the group. They were too focused on getting new members and on squeezing as much money from everyone as they could, rather than on helping people and spreading spiritual information. Timothy also said that he didn't think it was proper for the leader to be driving one of the most expensive luxury cars made, bought with the membership's money. The leader became angry and told Timothy to get out of the group immediately.

Timothy went home and thought about what had happened. He believed that he could begin his own group which would be far more successful than the one from which he had just been dismissed. And do it in a such a way that would be more nearly on the spiritual path.

He owned a building in the center of town that had a ground floor vacancy. He thought it would make a fine meeting hall. He decided to call it, "The Center." Timothy had a list of the members of the group he had just left and their telephone numbers. He spent the next three days calling them. He received a favorable response from some of the members, but from others he received an angry response. The leader of the organization heard about what Timothy was doing, called him, and threatened him with bodily harm if he didn't stop calling the members.

Timothy did a reading. His question was, "What can I expect from using The Center for a meeting hall to start my own spiritual group?" His answer was Kua 50, Ting, The Cauldron. The text of Kua 50 reads:

Ting is the symbol of the cauldron from which spiritual wisdom and information are dispensed. Ting is formed of the trigram of Li (intelligence and clarity) and Sun (penetrating wind). Together they create penetrating intelligence of a divine nature, which is dispensed from the cauldron. This kua brings supreme good fortune and success. By acting with divine wisdom and intelligence, the superior person creates a life of good fortune and success.

Timothy was exceptionally pleased with his answer. It answered his question perfectly and was a symbol of great good fortune.

There were two moving lines in the answer, 4 and 5. Line
4 reads:

**You have been assigned a difficult task, which you
attack too forcefully, causing damage to those
around you. Misfortune.**

Timothy could understand that. He had caused a lot of
problems by the way he had started. He realized that he should
have been much more discreet and called only those people he
felt were sympathetic toward his starting a new group.

Line 5 reads:

**You achieve a leading position and yet remain
modest and approachable, demonstrating a fine
understanding of universal law. To persist in such
manners and behavior will benefit you.**

Timothy understood that since Line 5 comes after Line
4, that it referred to a point in time later than that of Line 4.
He believed that Line 4 was applicable to the way he began
and that Line 5 applied to what was to come. He resolved to
follow the advice given in Line 5, in that he would always remain modest and approachable.

By virtue of the moving Lines, 4 and 5, the new kua was
37, Chia Jên, The Family, The Group. Kua 37 reads:

This kua depicts the inner structure and workings of a family unit or of an organization. When all the members of the family or organization fulfill their respective duties, showing one another the love and respect due to each of them, then the family or organization functions efficiently and harmoniously. A superior person has substance in his words, meaning that he does as he says he will do and speaks the truth. He cultivates duration in his way of life, meaning that he perseveres in walking a virtuous path, he does not change with every passing fad, and he is constant in his loyalty and dedication to the group.

Timothy told me that he was so overwhelmed with the accuracy of the reading and the perfect guidance given to him that he cried. Timothy's group fared extremely well, while his old group diminished slowly and went out of existence a year later. Chance meetings such as the one described between myself and Timothy in the final paragraph of this story seem to be coincidental—they are not. All is just as it should be. The sanest person comes to terms with that as early as possible, and as a result, enjoys a life of good fortune and happiness.

The Recluse

An old friend, Gertrude, asked me to go with her to visit a woman who was celebrating her seventieth birthday. I went. The woman, Mrs. Weatherstone, was a regal lady, very wealthy, who lived alone but for a servant and the maid who came in to care for the house. She had been a part of a large family and, while her husband and father were still alive, had participated in a great number of social events. Her husband had died twenty years earlier. Her father survived her husband by ten years. Before her husband died, she was the head of several charities and gave freely of her time and energy to worthy causes. She was fully involved, well liked, and highly respected. After her husband died, she participated in fewer endeavors but was still active. After her father died, she declined to participate in any social functions and gradually stopped all charitable activities. During the last four or five years, she had become quite reclusive.

There were only a few people at the subdued party, and everyone except Gertrude and I left after a couple of hours. We were sitting on an outdoor patio, having tea when

Gertrude told Mrs. Weatherstone of my interest in the I Ching. Mrs. Weatherstone commented that she had heard of the I Ching but didn't believe in any such hocus pocus. I laughed and said that she was not alone in her belief that being able to communicate with All-That-Is was simply a diversion of the empty-headed. We talked for a while about the I Ching. I told her of its great history and some of the learned minds that gave great credibility to that great old book and to our inherent ability to communicate with the intelligence of the Universe. She asked for a demonstration. I always travel with an *I Ching*, yarrow stalks, and incense, and so I went to my car and procured the necessary items and returned to the patio.

I asked Mrs. Weatherstone to get a pencil and paper and write a question that was uppermost in her mind. She wrote, "What can you tell me about me?" We lit the incense, passed all the items through the smoke three times, including our hands, then I guided her through the process of manipulating the yarrow stalks and her answer was Kua 48, Ching, The Well. The text of Kua 48 reads:

> The Well is the symbol of the unchangeable,
> inexhaustible abundance of the Universe. It is the
> spiritual source of nourishment and wisdom from
> which all can draw. In individual situations, the

source can stand for a well, a government, a teaching, information, a person or group, or any object under consideration which is a source. If those who draw from the source draw an insufficient amount, or if they fail in their efforts, misfortune results. The superior person encourages others to draw from the source and urges them to help one another in drawing from it.

It was clear to Mrs. Weatherstone that the text described her. She had been a great source of spiritual and financial nourishment for many people and groups for many years but had withdrawn into seclusion. No one sought her out any more, and she was lonely. I informed Mrs. Weatherstone about the moving lines and the way they took precedence over the reading, that the opening paragraph of a kua described the situation surrounding the question, and that if there were any moving lines, they gave specific direction for proceeding and further clarified the situation.

In her case, there were two moving lines, the bottom line and Line 5. The bottom line reads:

The source is muddy; therefore, it is of no use to anyone, and none avail themselves of it. Its time of usefulness may be past.

Mrs. Weatherstone was so moved by those words that she began to cry. Through her tears she told us that after her husband and father died, she felt as if she had dried up inside, that there was nothing left inside to give to anyone. I explained that Line 5, which was also a moving line, came after the bottom line in terms of time, and was a message of great hope and consolation for the days to come. The text of Line 5 reads:

> **Here, in the place of the leader, the source is**
> **pure and readily available so that everyone can**
> **be nourished.**

I added that Line 5 meant that she was not dried up inside at all, that she was obviously a source that was pure and readily available to nourish people, and in great abundance, and all she had to do was to make them aware of it. She must get out of the house and back into the mainstream of life. I told her about the changing lines creating a new kua that foretold what would happen for following the advice in the first kua. In this case Kua 48 became Kua 11, T'ai, Peaceful Prosperity, Harmony, Heaven on Earth. I read to her the text of Kua 11:

> **This kua is formed of the upper trigram of Earth,**
> **whose motion is downward, and the lower trigram**

of Heaven, whose motion is upward. The two come together, forming the condition of heaven on earth. The light force is in the ascendancy, and the dark force is diminishing. People in high places are considerate of their subordinates, and subordinates are respectful and helpful to those in power. It is a time when feuds end and friendships renew. Harmony prevails; pettiness ends. People act from their higher natures rather than from their lower. There is perfect correspondence in all areas, meaning that everyone gets along with everyone else. It is a time of good fortune and success, a time when small efforts bring large rewards. This time of harmony can be lengthened by healing dissension, making an extra effort to get along with others, being extra courteous and considerate, and participating in every way that is in accord with this time of Heaven on Earth.

Those words were a cause for a fresh outburst of tears from Mrs. Weatherstone. I told her of others who had followed the counsel they had received in readings and of the great successes they had achieved. We left Mrs. Weatherstone in a happy state of mind, filled with new plans for the future. That was seven years ago. Today Mrs. Weatherstone is the leading light in her city, and her social functions are reported in the newspapers, her charities are the talk of the county, and she is a happy woman who looks and acts ten years younger. Strangely enough, she has never done another I Ching reading. Recently we saw each other out walking and I asked her why and she said, "That one was enough to last me a lifetime."

Bashful Rob

A young man, Brian, took one of my one-day workshops on using the I Ching some years ago. He later told me the very interesting story that follows. I contacted his friend, Rob, about whom the story revolves, and had several discussions with him also. Both young men asked that their story be included in this book. I believe their stories are inspiring, enlightening, and make enjoyable reading.

Rob Howard was still shy as he prepared to begin his senior year in high school. Shyness had plagued him all through grammar school, junior high, his sophomore and junior years of high school, and still he was faced with it at the start of his senior year. He had no difficulty in associating with the people he knew well, his immediate circle of friends and his family; it was just new people that he had difficulty in meeting and communicating with freely. It was true that he was not as shy as he used to be, but he still had difficulty talking to girls, and he hated giving speeches in class or being the center of attention. As for getting up in front of a large group and speaking, it was his worst nightmare, even though he had never done it.

For all that, he was well-liked. He was modest, considerate of others, and he was always ready to lend a hand when it was needed.

Rob's dad had died when Rob was in the first grade, so he had always talked with his mother about his "growing-up" problems, shyness being chief among them. She had always said the same thing: "To learn to overcome shyness, go out and meet people. Just walk right up to them and introduce yourself." Rob couldn't do that. It was more difficult for him than his mother knew.

There was another complication. Rob's dad had been the mayor of the town, and from the time he was little, Rob had wanted to be mayor too, just like his dad. Now that his father was dead, Rob's dream was more important to him than ever. It was as if in becoming mayor, he would honor his father in some way. It was a way of keeping his dad's memory alive. His desire, coupled with his shyness, put a pressure on him that never seemed to let up. It wasn't a sharp pressure; it was just that it was always there.

At breakfast, on the morning he was leaving for his first day of high school, he said to his mother as he was walking out the door, "Well, here I go, bashful Robby, off to the first day of my senior year." His mother laughed, waved good-bye to him and called out jokingly, "Try running for class president."

After school that day he went to visit his friend, Brian. Brian had just taken a one-day workshop on the I Ching that

I conducted. He had learned how to manipulate the yarrow stalks and was eager to try it out again. He told Rob of the question he had asked in the workshop and how the answer had seemed exactly right. Brian asked Rob if he'd like to try it.

Of course, Rob's question was: "What can I do to overcome my shyness?" The answer was Kua 13, T'ung Jên, Socializing. Rob and Brian both laughed when they saw the answer because it summed up what Rob's mother had been telling Rob for years about how to overcome his shyness. The text of Kua 13 reads:

> This is the kua of people mingling openly. During this time of mingling, you will benefit if you join with others or organize others and then undertake some great endeavor. In fulfilling this achievement, you must be virtuous in your conduct, and you must act in the best interests of the group. Your correct action brings success.

Rob told Brian what his mother had jokingly said to him as he had left the house that morning, "Run for class president." He told Brian that maybe it wasn't such a bad idea, although the thought of it was terrifying to him. Brian told Rob about moving lines and said that Rob's reading had one, Line 2. The text of Line 2 reads:

> You are allowing yourself to associate only with
> those in your immediate circle. Continuing to do so
> will lead to embarrassment.

Rob was amazed at the perception of the reading. He said it gave him goose bumps it was so pertinent.

Brian explained to Rob about the second kua, created by the moving line or lines of the first kua. Kua 13, by virtue of Line 2 being a moving line, became Kua 1, Ch'ien, Creating. The text of Kua 1 reads:

> This is the kua of creating yourself as an individual
> or creating something of which you conceive. Enor-
> mous potential exists here. Follow the six steps of
> creation as indicated in the lines below to achieve
> the greatest possible success and to avoid failure.
> Since all the lines of the kua are strong, light-giving,
> good lines, perseverance in a virtuous course of
> action is essential. For acting in accordance with
> that which is highest and best within you, sublime
> success that comes from the primal depths of the
> Universe is assured. Great good fortune.

Rob was, to use his words, "blown away," by the reading. He was elated to think that there was a way he could make contact with the Universe and actually get answers. He was also excited by the prospect of actually overcoming his shyness, and in just the way his mother had counseled him. He wanted to ask another question. Brian agreed, and Rob's second question was, "What can I expect if I run for class president?" The answer was Kua 35, Chin, Great Progress. There were no moving lines. The text of Kua 35 reads:

> Great achievements can now be accomplished, and great merit will be richly rewarded. During this time of rapid, easy progress, pay great attention to brightening your virtues and being certain your actions are based on what is right and just. Pay strict attention to following a virtuous course of action, and your success is assured.

Rob later told me that with butterflies in his stomach at the thought of what he was about to undertake, he decided at that moment to run for class president.

Brian said that before Rob actually declared to the student body that he was running for the office of president, that he should do another reading and ask what he could do to achieve success. They did the reading and the answer was Kua 7, Shih, Collective Forces. The text of Kua 7 reads:

> When a large group of people is brought together, whether by design or accident, achieving success

and good fortune requires a strong leader and strict discipline. This is true of an army, a social or political organization, a public or private gathering, even a mob. For the mass to be effective, its members must be controlled, for they can then act in concert. The leader gains control by providing clear-cut, worthy goals to which individuals can dedicate themselves, thereby awakening the group's enthusiasm. If the leader is not the ultimate authority, those in the position of ultimate authority must give the leader their full confidence, total authority to act in their behalf, and complete support.

The bottom line was a moving line. The text of the bottom line reads:

In this time of beginning, as in all beginnings, exceptional care must be exercised if the desired end is to be reached. Order must prevail from the outset. The plan must be complete and clear, the group highly organized, the assets in place, and the goal just. Because in this instance there is a certain weakness present, a double measure of caution is required.

After reading the text of the bottom line, Brian told me that Rob had thrown back his head and screamed, "I can't believe it! This is so right on! It even knows about my weakness!" Brian wanted to see what the kua became by virtue of its moving line. They looked it up on the chart and found that Kua 7 became Kua 19, Lin, Advancing, Progress. The text of Kua 19 reads:

> During this propitious time, your advance will be crowned with supreme success. You must act swiftly and make the best use of the time, for the time of rapid, easy advance does not last forever. The ancient text reads that the superior man is inexhaustible in his teaching and that his tolerance of the people and his protection of them know no limits.

Rob announced his candidacy the next day, and said that his friend, Brian, was to be his campaign manager.

Rob said that the counsel of Kua 7 said that the leader who wanted to gain control of a group, in his case students, had to provide clear-cut, worthy goals to which his followers could dedicate themselves. Therefore, the first thing he had to do was create a campaign platform. With that in mind, he enlisted the aid of several friends to circulate among the student body to discover what changes the students wanted for their school. Rob talked to the faculty and staff to see what it was that they wanted in the way of changes or reforms. The first thing Brian had to do as campaign manager was to get himself a core group of helpers.

It was time for Brian to ask a question. His question was: "What do I have to know about getting campaign helpers?" The answer was Kua 8, Pi, Joining, Supporting, Uniting. The text of Kua 8 reads:

> Joining, supporting, or uniting individuals into a group brings good fortune because members of the group support each other. Waiting too long to join, support, or gather a group brings danger. Inquire of the oracle again to see what area of self development will now be of greatest benefit to you in attaining your goal.

The reading had one moving line, 2. The text of Line 2 reads:

> You are in a minor position of authority and have a good relationship with the leader. Remain inwardly true to the leader, be cautious in your outward behavior, and good fortune will prevail.

The kua, by virtue of its moving line, became Kua 2, K'un, Open, Receptive, Yielding, Willing to Follow. The text of Kua 2 reads:

> The greatest possible success, sublime success, is obtainable if you are willing to follow good counsel, to

be open and receptive to new information, to be willing to yield to the ideas and wishes of others, to be willing to follow those virtuous people whose goals are worthy, to work hard, to cooperate, and to avoid being an arrogant leader. If you can find like-minded people to help, join them or encourage them to join you; if not, carry on alone. Success is assured.

Brian could not have been happier with his reading. Because the text of Kua 8 had counseled him to make another inquiry regarding self-development, he did. Brian's question was: "What area of self development will now be of greatest benefit to me in being a good campaign manager?" the answer was Kua 20, Kuan, Looking Inward, Seeing the World Outwardly, Being Looked Up To as an Example. The text of Kua 20 reads:

This kua takes its meaning from what it resembles: a tall tower. The four lower divided lines represent the legs, and the top two undivided lines represent the platform. Standing on this tall tower, one can see far away and be seen from far away, which gives rise to being looked up to as an example. The upper trigram, Sun, symbolized by the gentle wind blowing over the Earth, penetrating every nook and cranny, shows what inner and outer seeing should be like; it misses nothing.

The third line in his reading was a moving line. The text of Line 3 reads:

> This is a time for you to examine yourself in great detail to see what you have accomplished, how you have affected others, and who you truly are. You are in a position to advance, but if you are unworthy, misfortune will result, and you should retreat to improve yourself. If your self-examination shows you to be worthy, your advance will be greatly successful.

Brian realized that he would be very visible to all his classmates and the faculty of the school during the election campaign. He understood that his reading was directing him to look carefully at himself and also at what he had accomplished in his lifetime. He must examine the ways others saw him and what effect he had upon them. If others whom he had influenced had been influenced for the good, he could advance swiftly and with great success. If poorly, then he had to make changes before he embarked on this task of campaign manager for his friend, or his efforts would end in failure for them both.

Brian began by examining his relationships as far back as he could remember. All of his friendships underwent his careful scrutiny. He remembered harmful things he had done to friends, taunts he had spoken in anger, mean things he had said that had hurt them. He knew that all children do that when they are growing up, but he looked at them in the context of his reading and learned from them. He also looked back and remembered the good things he had done. Help he had rendered to his friends when they needed it, favors he had done for them when he could, and he felt he had certainly done more good than bad. He looked at what he had just done for his friend Rob. He had shown him how to use the I Ching, he had helped him to reach a decision to overcome his shyness, and he would help him to become class president. All in all, he felt that he had come to understand himself, perhaps to see himself as if from a distance, as others saw him, and he had gained from the experience. He was ready to go ahead with his plans.

As a result of Line 3's being a moving line, Kua 20 became Kua 53, Chien, Gradual Development. The text of Kua 53 reads:

> This kua shows the process of things that develop slowly and as a consequence become strong and enduring. Because gradual development requires extended time, perseverance is required so that the development continues and does not slow or stop altogether. By adhering to good values and right conduct during this time of gradual development, you will set a good example for others and enjoy long lasting success and good fortune.

Brian set the goal of adhering to strong principles firmly in his mind. He was going to run the cleanest, most honorable campaign he could.

Brian and Rob worked hard. They continued to talk to their classmates, teachers, and other members of the staff to see what they would like from a class president. As a result, they were able to modify their already strong platform to make it even stronger. They also gathered a few dedicated helpers to assist them.

When the campaign was well under way and they were approaching the election, Rob and Brian sat down one night to assess their progress. They were concerned that because of the great popularity of Rob's opponent, they might not be leading the race and might need a new strategy.

Rob's opponent was captain of the football team, and a very popular boy he was. His campaign team was made up of other popular football players and some of the cheerleaders. He had been referring to Rob as a wallflower, a bashful baby who had trouble getting up in front of a group to make a speech. He told the student body that if they elected Rob president, he wouldn't accomplish anything for them, whereas he, the leader of the football team, the aggressive, dynamic captain, who was leading his team to an undefeated season, would accomplish great deeds for them.

Rob thought that he should start campaigning in the same way his opponent was campaigning. Rob knew he was a lot smarter than him and earned much better grades. Perhaps he should start talking about his opponent as a stupid gorilla, a know-nothing whose only use was to butt heads on the football field.

Rob and Brian decided to do a reading. They rightfully thought it could be confusing to do a joint reading, so Rob did one on his own but with Brian present. Rob's question was: "How am I doing with regard to the election?" The answer was Kua 14, Ta Yu, Great Abundance, Great Wealth. The text of Kua 14 reads:

This is the kua of great wealth that has already been accumulated. Its lines provide guidance for proper conduct in such a condition. By eliminating evil influences in your life and propagating good influences, you put yourself in accord with the highest universal principles, which bring supreme success as a result of the fulfillment of natural law.

Rob and Brian believed that the great wealth that had already been accumulated was the confidence and support of their classmates which was being demonstrated to them every day on campus. They felt as if they were conducting a good campaign, honest and forthright without any mud-slinging, and that they had addressed the concerns of the students, the faculty, and the staff alike. Rob asked his question with the idea

of changing tactics to those of his opponent, but his interpretation of the reading led him to believe that they were doing fine in conducting the campaign in the current manner.

The reading had a moving line, 5. The text reads:

> You have attained the place of the leader and have
> amassed great wealth, yet you have remained
> modest; therefore, you are well liked and respected,
> and your followers find it easy to deal with you.
> You do not take advantage of anyone; your sincerity
> is your hallmark, and you maintain excellent relation-
> ships with your followers. By keeping yourself
> dignified and your wisdom simple, you will have
> good fortune.

The course of action they were to follow could not have
been laid out any clearer. They were to maintain a clean campaign, free of dirty politics. Kua 14, by virtue of its moving line,
changed into Kua 1, Ch'ien, Creating. The text of Kua 1 reads:

> This is the kua of creating yourself as an individual
> or creating something of which you conceive. Enor-
> mous potential exists here. Follow the six steps of
> creation as indicated in the lines below to achieve
> the greatest possible success and to avoid failure.
> Since all the lines of the kua are strong, light-giving,

good lines, perseverance in a virtuous course of
action is essential. For acting in accordance with
that which is highest and best within you, sublime
success that comes from the primal depths of the
Universe is assured. Great good fortune.

That convinced them. They would not resort to the
mud-slinging tactics of Rob's opponent, but would keep
steadily on with their campaign which was based on what
was good for the students, faculty, and staff. Looming on the
horizon, only one week away, were the campaign speeches
to be delivered by the two candidates before the entire student body. Rob knew on that day he would be faced with the
greatest test of his life; he would have to confront his dead-
liest fear. He concentrated all his efforts on writing his speech
and preparing himself for that day. He invited his mother
and several of her friends because he wanted her there
whichever way he performed, brilliantly or disastrously.

This was not only going to be the deciding factor in the
election; it was also going to be the test to see whether in his
weeks of campaigning he had gained enough confidence
to overcome his embarrassment in speaking to a group of
people. He had never gotten up in front of a group as large
as the student body before, some 1500 students and faculty,
and he was extremely nervous. His mother was already proud
of him for what he had accomplished, and she said that she

was sure he would do just fine. Rob wasn't so sure. In fact, he was terrified.

He did a reading. His question was, "What can I expect as a result of debating with the football captain in front of the whole school?" The answer was Kua 16, Yü, Enthusiasm, Revelry, Celebration. The text of Kua 16 reads:

> Thunder resounding joyfully from the earth indicates enthusiasm and revelry. In times of such great enthusiasm, one may easily enlist the aid of helpers and set them to work.

The moving line was 4. The text of Line 4 reads:

> You are the inspiration of celebration and enthusiasm for those around you. This is a time when you easily attract helpers. Do not hold any doubts about your abilities or actions. Success is assured, and you will accomplish great deeds.

Rob was overjoyed at the words and felt much better. He interpreted the part of the reading about enlisting the aid of helpers and being able to attract helpers as obtaining the support of the student voters. Kua 16, by virtue of its moving line, became Kua 2, K'un, Open, Receptive, Yielding, Willing to Follow. The text of Kua 2 reads:

The greatest possible success, sublime success, is obtainable if you are willing to follow good counsel, to be open and receptive to new information, to be willing to yield to the ideas and wishes of others, to be willing to follow those virtuous people whose goals are worthy, to work hard, to cooperate, and to avoid being an arrogant leader. If you can find like-minded people to help, join them or encourage them to join you; if not, carry on alone. Success is assured.

With those words of assurance, most of Rob's apprehensions left him. He worked hard on his speech and when the time came for the debate, he felt tense, but ready.

His opponent spoke to the assembly first. He spent a good part of his speech running Rob down to the students. He told them that Rob was so shy that he actually might not even talk that day, and he was so timid that he wouldn't be able to accomplish anything for them. Next, he spent time building himself up; then he told them what he would do for them if he was elected president. He told several funny jokes and had the students laughing hard. There was no doubt that he was a very popular young man.

Rob's turn came. He took a deep breath and walked to the center of the stage. He looked around at the huge crowd and began to get very nervous. Then he remembered the reading, which he had memorized. The words came easily to his mind:

You are the inspiration of celebration and enthusiasm for those around you. This is a time when you easily attract helpers. Do not hold any doubts about your abilities or actions. Success is assured, and you will accomplish great deeds.

Then he began to speak. He told the students, faculty, and the scattering of parents who were in attendance, that it was true that he was shy. It was true that he was timid. Or at least that he had been shy and timid at the beginning of the year. Yet here he was, standing in front of them all, running for the office of class president. It was also true, he told them, that at that moment he was very nervous and, he wiped his brow with a handkerchief, very wet with perspiration. Yet, he said, here I am, addressing you.

He stopped to let that sink in. At first there was only silence. Then there was a small bit of applause, and then it caught on, and soon students were on their feet, cheering and clapping. When the room was quiet, he told them that what he had done, they could do, that his victory was their victory. He made them the winners along with himself. While he spoke, the last of his nervousness disappeared, and he delivered an effective and stirring speech, never once speaking badly about his opponent. Quite the reverse, he said to them that if it was their choice to elect the football captain instead of him, that he was sure that he would also do an admirable job. At that, there was more applause. He told them that the greatest chore that faces any of us is living up to our potential and overcoming our fears. He said that anyone who could do that could do anything.

The next day, election day, Rob won by a large margin. He and Brian had won a great victory, not just of the election, but over themselves. They celebrated with their helpers and well-wishers, and Rob vowed to fulfill his campaign promises. Rob's mother cried. The football captain sought him out and, in a private conversation, congratulated Rob on his excellent campaign. He said that he had learned a lot from it and was going to use Rob as his inspiration to lead a better life. It was a great time for them all.

Later that night, when Rob was at home in his room by himself, he took down from the shelf his new copy of the *I Ching* and took it out of its silk wrapping. He held it high over his head and spoke aloud to All-That-Is: "Thanks a lot," was all he said. Then he looked at a favorite picture of his dad and said: "If you can hear me, Dad, that win was for you. It was my first step toward becoming mayor of our town. Thanks for the inspiration."

The Traveler

The son of the man in the following story wrote to me to tell me that his father had asked him to find me and thank me for writing my books on the I Ching, and to let me know how they had helped him in his final days. I listened to the story and was very moved by it. I told the young man I was going to write this book, and he gave me permission to include his father's story.

Mr. Farnsworth was ill. Very ill. He had been told by his doctors that he had cancer and was dying. They said he had a few months at best. It was a difficult prognosis for Mr. Farnsworth to accept. He didn't want to die; he wanted to live. He had things he wanted to do, places he wanted to go, friends he hadn't seen for years that he wanted to visit, and, being a wealthy man, many business interests and holdings that were not in order because he thought there was plenty of time for everything he wanted to do. If he died now, much of what he had worked for all his life would be lost, and his family would never be able to sort through it all. He became very angry and abusive to nearly everyone, including his family, even though they all loved him and had been very supportive of him.

His will was not made, and the family trust he had planned to set up was not done either. His wife went to the hospital and asked him to attend to all the things he needed to do to prepare for his death, but he became enraged and told her to get out of his room. His three children tried to talk to him, to calm him, but he was so angry at having to die just at that time, before he had done the things he wanted to do, that he was inconsolable. Besides that, he didn't believe the doctors. He was ill, that much was certain, but he felt that he could live at least ten more years.

His oldest son, who knew that his father used the I Ching, reminded him that he could ask questions and have them answered in a way that might help him through this troubled time. Upon hearing that, Mr. Farnsworth brightened considerably and asked that the *I Ching* and the yarrow stalks be brought to him along with paper, pencil, incense, and matches. He asked to be left alone. He wrote out his question. It was: "What can I do to regain my health?" The answer was Kua 56, Lü, The Wanderer, The Traveler. The text of 56 reads:

> The kua depicts a stranger or one who travels. In either case, the visit is temporary and, therefore, only limited progress can be made. Lofty goals or goals

that can only be obtained through perseverance should not be undertaken for you will not tarry long. You must act with reserve, virtue, and modesty while refraining from all aggressive behavior if you are to attain even the small progress possible. If any disputes arise, settle them quickly and be cautious in imposing penalties.

When Mr. Farnsworth read that, he understood without a doubt that his time on Earth was short, maybe even shorter than the doctors thought. He immediately lost all his feelings of anger and disappointment. The next morning he called his lawyer, had his will updated, had a trust created, and began to put his affairs in order. He worked every day for three weeks, during which time he patched up all his family quarrels and returned to the role of the loving, caring, husband and father he had always been. He spent quality time with his wife, children, and grandchildren. His affairs were almost in order when he took a turn for the worse. He had a final meeting with his family in which he told them all how much he loved them, and a few hours later he went into a coma and died that same afternoon. When his family came to take his personal belongings home with them, they found a last note he had written that morning. It was dated and signed. It said,

"Every ending contains a new beginning.

In *I Ching Wisdom* it reads:

Every person
must have something to follow,
a lodestar.

Wu Wei's comment:
Everyone needs something to bring out the best in himself and to provide direction for his development. By holding the image of the superior person in your mind as your lodestar, you will achieve not only supreme success but also great happiness.

In the last chapter of *I Ching Life*, I listed some of the characteristics of the superior person, meaning a person who acts with worthy motives, who strives to be the best person possible. I list those characteristics here again for your consideration. See page 271.

Free Will

During 1986, the woman in this story wrote to me and asked several questions about life after death, free will, and reincarnation. I suggested that she do several readings and suggested the questions to her. She was kind enough to share her answers and thoughts with me so I can share them with you.

Marie, a physicist in Santa Fe, New Mexico wanted to know whether or not there was such a thing as free will. Her question was, "What can you tell me about whether or not we have free will?" Her answer was Kua 60, Chieh, Setting Limitations. The text of Kua 60 reads:

> To live the life of the superior person, enjoying the rewards that accompany such a life, you must limit your activities, your thoughts, your associations, your eating and drinking, your sleeping, working, carousing, spending, amassing, and, in fact, every aspect of your life. Everything in moderation benefits you; the same thing carried to excess destroys you. Therefore, this kua cautions you to limit

everything to its most beneficial level but not to so severely limit yourself or others that the limitations become abusive and detrimental. That kind of moderation brings success. Define for yourself the kind of life you want to have and the best ways to achieve that life using limitation to avoid excesses. Have a clearly defined idea about what your conduct should be and what degree of virtue you wish to attain to.

Marie interpreted her answer to mean that she had free will, but that to experience the best that life had to offer, the essence of life, and to be successful, she should voluntarily put limitations on herself. She would not eat or drink too much, sleep too much, play too much, work too much, travel too much, or over-indulge in any activity that would be detrimental to well-being. Even in her topics of study she would limit herself so that she would be able to attain depth in a particular field, rather than study so widely that she would not achieve depth in any field. She would also limit her spending so that she would never be in want. Marie interpreted her answer to mean that she had free will to do as she wished within the scope of her capabilities, but that she should set limitations for herself within which she would experience complete freedom, and thereby attain success and happiness.

Marie asked that question in 1986. She reports that she has experienced great rewards for following the path she chose for herself, and that she believes that we have free will to do as we want within the scope of our capabilities.

Shock!

The following story happened to me in 1993 and provided me with a great gift and a deep understanding of Kua 51 Chên, Shock, The Arousing.

My son, Pax, and I had gone to a mountain to collect rocks for a garden. It was early in the morning and the dew was still on the ground when we arrived in my old truck at the base of the mountain. I followed a winding dirt road that led around the base of the mountain till I reached an area where there was a deep ravine at the side of the road. There I saw part of an interesting rock protruding from the ground at the edge of the ravine. I stopped the truck and got out and walked over to the edge of the ravine. From that vantage point, I could see the depth of the rock, which was about twenty inches, and it appeared to be about a foot thick. It looked as if it weighed about 175 pounds. What made the rock interesting to me was its shape, which was like that of a pyramid, but with many protrusions and different angles.

The ravine at that point was about thirty feet deep. The sides of the ravine were quite steep. I carefully climbed down into the ravine and began to dig around the rock with a small pick to loosen it from its place. Pax walked along the ravine searching for other rocks. I was wearing tai chi shoes with cotton soles and therefore did not have much gripping power on the moist dirt. After I had cleared enough dirt from the rock so that there was a place underneath where I could push up on it, I used my pick to dig small shelves into the side of the ravine so I would have a firm footing, then I laid my pick aside and placed my hands on the bottom of the rock to roll it up and onto the road. I began to apply pressure to the base of the rock and it slowly came loose from its place. I could feel the weight of the rock pushing my feet into the soil as I slowly lifted it upward until it was at the top ready to roll onto the road; it was nearly at the balance point, when just another small effort would send it toppling onto the road, but the earth gave way beneath my feet, and I slid quite fast to the bottom of the ravine. I managed to keep my balance and remained standing. I was leaning forward with my arms outstretched against the side of the ravine, supporting myself as if I were doing a vertical push up, when the rock came hurtling down the ravine. It crashed onto the top of my head with such force that it drove me to the ground hard enough to break two small bones in my hand, raise welts on my knees, and smash four disks in my neck. The sharp crack of the rock hitting my head sounded as if a baseball bat had been broken.

I rolled over onto my back in the cool mud, a profusion of blood running onto my face, and wondered why I was still conscious. I couldn't imagine being hit so hard and still being alive. I was afraid to reach up and explore the wound with my hand because I believed I would put my finger into the hole I knew must be in my skull and touch my brain and kill myself. The very next thought that came to my mind was, "I wonder what good thing will come from this?" I was certain that the so-called accident was entirely for my benefit, and I silently acknowledged the gift. Finally, I reached up and felt the wound, which was a gash about two inches long, and discovered that my skull was solid underneath. Of course, blood was everywhere.

Pax came running up to me, horrified by the blood running down my face and from seeing me lying, unmoving, in the mud, and he knelt down and I opened my eyes. He asked me if I was all right. I said I didn't know, but that we should wait quietly for a while and we would see.

I lay there wondering why I had no pain, why I was not dead, and why I was conscious. I could only conclude that it was some wonderful gift from the Universe and that all would be revealed to me in time. After a time I was able to move, and Pax assisted me out of the ravine and drove me home. I stood under a shower and let the water trickle onto my wound to cleanse it. Then I went to bed to rest with ice on top of my head. Later, Pax drove me to our family doctor's office and I had my scalp stitched together. I remember that during the time my scalp was being stitched and later when I was recuperating, I was wondering what good thing I could expect as a result of being hit by the rock. It never once occurred to me that it was bad luck, that I had been ill-used, or that something bad would come from the event.

I knew that being a part of the Universe, whatever happens to me happens for my complete benefit. I wondered what the gift of the rock was.

I did go back—with helpers—to get the rock for my garden. Two weeks later I was sitting in my garden reading the *I Ching* when I glanced up at the rock. I again wondered what that event had meant to me. I had heard of other people who sustained head injuries who gained great mental powers as a result of their injuries. I did an I Ching reading to discover what the reason was behind my getting hit on the head. I didn't quite know how to phrase the question so I wrote, "I want to know about the rock hitting my head." The answer was Kua 51, Chên, Shock, The Arousing. The text of Kua 51 reads:

> Shock! A manifestation of God. It usually causes fear and trembling, but the superior person does not let the shock drive from his mind the awareness that he is a divine creature in a divine Universe and that the shock was entirely for his benefit. He retains his rev-

erence for All-That-Is. Such reverence brings success.
After sustaining a shock, the superior person examines his life to see whether he is a good person and
accomplishing good things. He then orders his life
according to the highest principles.

I still didn't know what the gift was, but I was supremely
pleased with the reading. It confirmed what I assumed, that
the event was a gift.

A few days later, I was studying a passage in the I Ching
that had long puzzled me when I realized I was no longer
puzzled. It was as if I had been looking at a collection of dots
that became a picture of my house. I was delighted to suddenly understand something which had eluded my com-
prehension for so many years. I was even more delighted a
few days later when that experience was repeated with another passage. I then turned quickly to other troublesome
parts of the I Ching, and one by one, they too were crystal
clear. It was then that I became aware what the gift of the
rock was. And what a gift! Especially for me who has sought
after the wisdom of the I Ching for decades and in whose
life the great book has played such an important role. The
rock crashing onto my head had opened channels in my
brain or in my mind which permitted me to have greater insight and understanding of the I Ching. I could only nod my
head and smile in silent appreciation of the great gift. What

a truly wonderful Universe we are part of. It is absolutely glorious. It is at moments like that when I feel great gratitude and love for All-That-Is. Even now, writing this many years later, I can again experience the moment of realization when I first perceived the great gift of the rock.

It was stated in the reading,

> He retains his reverence for All-That-Is. Such reverence brings success.

I believe it was because I kept the awareness, even as I lay in the mud with blood running onto my face, that the rock hitting me was not an unfortunate accident but a real gift, that the gift was received.

The way we respond to events determines their outcome in our lives. Had I cursed my ill-fortune, become angry and ill-tempered, I probably would not have received the gift at all. In that case, it would most likely have been better for me, cosmically speaking, that the rock had been an eviction notice from the planet.

Time for a Change

The girl in this story took one of my classes several years ago. In the class, told me she was going through a problem with her husband. I helped her to phrase a few questions she could ask and gave her my telephone number in case she had further questions. A few months later, she called and told me the story that follows.

Wilhelmina describes herself as "plain." She has brown hair and eyes, is of average height, has a sprinkling of freckles across her nose, and keeps herself in good physical condition. She describes her physical condition as "trim." Her friends call her Willi.

Willi married Burt when she was twenty-two. He was four years older than she, and for the first couple of years everything went rather well, except that it became evident to Willi after a few months of marriage that Burt didn't have much respect for women. That was evidenced by the disparaging remarks he made about women in general, particularly when he became angry. He also had a nasty temper, but since she was easygoing and careful, they only quarreled occasionally, which Willi thought was natural for couples to do. Willi tried to talk to him about his attitude regarding women, but he only laughed and said that she couldn't help trying to stand up for her half of the human race, but then, she was only a woman and what could one expect. Willi refused to let his attitude about women upset her, and believed that in time she would be able to change the way he thought.

They had a nice apartment in a good part of town, they each had a car, and they both worked. Willi was a secretary in a law firm, and Burt was an auto mechanic, but was studying for entrance into the police academy. On weekends they went hiking or camped out in a forest about two hours away from their home.

Sometime during the middle of the third year of their marriage, Burt began to treat Willi differently. He wasn't as nice to her as he had been earlier. His disrespect for women was becoming more and more evident in the way he was treating her. Sometimes he'd stay out late drinking beer with his buddies and when he came home he wouldn't say where he'd been. Willi thought it was a phase he was going through and that it would pass, but it didn't. Burt became more difficult, stayed out more, and occasionally didn't come home at all. Willi tried to talk to him, but all he'd say was that it was none of her business where he went or what he did.

Willi talked to Burt's parents, Harry and Gail, but to no avail. They didn't know what to do either. It seemed to

Willi as if Burt's father secretly approved of the way Burt was treating her, and on two occasions she saw him treating his wife in much the same way Burt was treating her.

One day Willi called Burt's mother and asked to meet with her privately. At lunch the next day, Willi told Gail that she suspected that Burt's father secretly admired Burt for the poor manner in which Burt was treating her. She asked Gail if she had ever been treated that way by her husband. Not surprisingly, Burt's mother said that she had been treated like that during her whole marriage, although Harry never did it in public, and it was her opinion that Burt was trying to be like his dad whom he greatly admired. Willi thanked Gail for her honesty and told her she'd keep their conversation confidential.

The next week Willi went to visit her own parents in the next town and told them about her situation at home and about Burt's parents, particularly what Burt's mother had told her about the way Burt's father treated his wife, and asked for their advice. Willi's mother was angry and said that Willi should leave Burt immediately and give him time to come to his senses. If he didn't come to his senses after the separation, Willi should get a divorce and find herself a new man. Life, she said, was too short to waste on people who didn't know how to treat each other. Willi's father was of a different opinion. He said Willi should get Burt into a therapy program right away. It was obvious to him that Burt's relationship with his father was a close one and that his father had set an extremely poor example for his son to follow. He said it was evident that Burt didn't respect women, and a good therapist might be able to help him. He advised Willi to adopt a "wait-and-see" attitude, but said she should take steps to correct the situation while she was waiting.

Willi had used the I Ching for several years while she was in college, but hadn't used it since she married and didn't know where it was. She went to her local bookstore to get another copy of the *I Ching* where, it so happened, I was giving a lecture. Willi attended the lecture and did a reading along with everyone else in the room. After the lecture, Willi sought me out, and we talked for awhile. She told me about the situation with her husband, and I asked her if that was what her question had been about during the lecture. She said it was. I asked what the question was specifically. She said she had asked, "What do I need to know about my husband, Burt?" Her answer was Kua 18, Ku, Correcting Deficiencies. The text of the kua reads:

> Whether what needs to be corrected is in yourself or outside yourself, careful planning is essential if the goal is to be reached. Once the corrective work has begun, careful monitoring is essential if the work is to proceed correctly and regression is not to set in. Enlist the aid of the people and lend

them encouragement. Your efforts will bring you
supreme success.

There is a note added to the end of the first paragraph
in my book that reads:

In the original text, lines one through five have to
do with correcting deficiencies that were caused by
either the mother or the father. Experience has
shown me that, in most cases, the use of mother
and father is metaphorical, meaning that the two
terms are symbols for something else. What that
something is can be determined from the conditions surrounding your question. Do not however
overlook the possibility that the guidance should be
taken literally, meaning the correction of deficiencies caused by the mother or the father.

In the case of Willi's husband, it was obvious that the
reading referred to deficiencies caused by the father. In Willi's
reading, Line 4 was a moving line. The text of Line 4 reads:

Tolerating deficiencies caused by the father: You
can see the deficiency, but to take action to correct
it at this time will be an error and will lead to
embarrassment.

It was clear that Willi was not to take any action to correct Burt's deficiency caused by his father. By virtue of Line 4 changing, the new kua was 50, The Cauldron. The text of Kua 50 reads:

Ting is the symbol of the cauldron from which spiritual wisdom and information are dispensed. Ting is formed of the trigram of Li (intelligence and clarity) and Sun (penetrating wind). Together they create penetrating intelligence of a divine nature, which is dispensed from the cauldron. This kua brings supreme good fortune and success. By acting with divine wisdom and intelligence, the superior person creates a life of good fortune and success.

The reading pinpointed the situation precisely: she should put up with the situation a while longer, and should not take any action at that time. I stated my belief that the portion of the reading having to do with "The Well" meant that by biding her time and not taking any action at that time, she would be become aware of information later that would be greatly helpful to her. I added that situations were always changing, and that what might not be a good move at that time might be a good move at another. She should wait, monitor the situation, and ask again when she thought it was appropriate. I suggested a few more questions she could ask and she left.

Willi was satisfied with the reading and decided that because the first part of her reading stated that she was to enlist the aid of people, she would seek counsel for herself from a professional. She found a therapist who specialized in marital problems and made an appointment. The counselor had two meetings with Willi and then asked her to bring Burt in to her office so she could talk with him. Willi thought about the reading she had obtained, particularly the text of Line 4 that had stated:

> **You can see the deficiency, but to take action to correct it at this time will be an error and will lead to embarrassment.**

She was a little embarrassed to tell the therapist that she didn't want to talk to Burt because of an I Ching reading, but she did. The therapist said that for her to refuse to bring Burt in to see her because of an I Ching reading was foolishness and that if Willi wanted her help she had to cooperate.

Willi did another reading. Her question was: "What should I do about following the therapist's advice to ask Burt to talk to her?" The answer was Kua 5, Hsü, Holding Back in the Face of Danger. The text of Line 5 reads:

This kua depicts a strong person below, who desires to advance, and grave danger above, which threatens the one who advances. To wait until the danger passes is the correct action, for to advance in the face of this great danger would be foolhardy. However, because the lower trigram is composed of three strong lines, the people or groups of people they represent will ultimately be successful in their advance, provided that they remain true to their natures, which are light-giving, pure, and virtuous. It will be of benefit to begin a major undertaking or journey when the time of waiting is past, whichever is called for. During the time of waiting, the superior person clarifies his plans, feasts, maintains a joyous and promising outlook, and is unconcerned, knowing he will ultimately reach his goal.

The answer was crystal clear. Willi was to wait. Any action taken at that time to get Burt into the therapist's office would result in grave danger.

Willi told the therapist about her reading and said that she believed in her readings and that if it was okay with the therapist, she would just wait. The therapist said that Willi's reliance on a Chinese fortune telling book was childish, and if Willi wanted to act in a sophisticated, twentieth century manner, she had to put her voodoo dolls away and act the part of an educated, liberated women.

Willi was reluctant to go against the counsel of the reading, but the therapist had been highly recommended, and she didn't want to appear foolish, so she went home and waited for Burt to arrive. She fixed him his favorite dinner, made him his favorite drink, and afterward she told Burt she had gone to a marriage therapist in town to see if she could get help for herself, to see if there was anything she was doing that was causing the problem between them. She told him that the therapist had asked if he would make an appointment to go in and talk to her.

Burt became extremely angry and began shouting at Willi. He accused her of telling the whole town about his personal life. He became very abusive in his language and told Willi that she must think he was sick and needed a doctor. "What the hell could you possibly have been thinking about?" he shouted. "Don't you know that because of what you have done the whole town will know that you're going to see a therapist, and the therapist will blab everything you've told her all over town and everyone will think I'm sick?" He screamed at her: "Just what in the hell is the matter with you anyway? Are you so stupid as all that?" The more he raged at her, the madder he became.

Willi pleaded with him not to get mad, that she was only trying to help their marriage. She said that she believed that the therapist could help. The more Willi tried to reason with him, the madder Burt became. Finally he worked himself into such a state that he began to beat Willi with his fists. She cried and pleaded with him to stop, but it was as if he had lost his mind, and he kept it up until she lost consciousness.

Willi awoke in the emergency ward of the local hospital. One of the neighbors in the apartment house had heard the screaming and called the police. They had come and arrested Burt and called an ambulance for Willi. She was checked over and released the next morning with some ugly bruises, a black eye, and a broken wrist. The therapist read of Willi's beating in the paper and called her. She was full of apologies for counseling her to act in a manner that ended so badly. Willi didn't want to talk to her and said so.

Burt was still in jail when Willi was released from the hospital the next day. She needed counseling, and badly. What should she do about her marriage? She got out her *I Ching* and yarrow stalks and even with her broken wrist in a cast, did a reading. The question she asked was: "What action should I take at this time regarding my marriage?" Her answer was Kua 49, Ko, Achievement. Willi read the text of Kua 49 with relief. It reads:

When the time for a change is at hand, you will inspire the confidence of those who will assist you in bringing about the change. By ceaselessly following a correct path, you will achieve supreme success, and all occasions for remorse will pass. It will benefit you and those around you to organize your schedules and carefully make plans for the coming change.

In Willi's reading, Line 2 was a moving line. Line 2 reads:

You have the necessary strength and clarity to bring about the required change, and you have the support of those in power. To begin at this time brings good fortune, and no blame will attach to your progress.

Willi believed that the support of those in power probably was referring to the divorce court or maybe her parents, who were now both very much in favor of Willi's separating herself from Burt forever.

Willi told me that she actually laughed when she read the kua that Kua 49 turned into by virtue of its moving line. It was Kua 43 Kuai, Overthrow of the Dark Force. The text of Kua 43 reads:

The five strong, virtuous lines below are mounting upward with inexorable force with the intent of overthrowing the last weak, evil line. The five lines represent five strong people, groups, or forces working together or the full force of your own personality or some other powerful forces that are rooted in righteousness and working as a team. Standing in the way of a complete takeover by the good and benevolent forces is a last evil line. It may be representative of a person at the top level of an organization, a final bad habit, a disruptive family member, a faction within a group, or another entity of the same nature. This solitary line seems gentle and meek, but its power is insidious, and it is at the height of influence. There is no question about the outcome; nothing will stop the advance of the five unbroken lines which are working in concert, but the overthrow of the last line must be accomplished in the right way. To resort to evil methods will make you an instrument and an ally of evil, and it will also increase the power of the remaining evil line, making its removal that much more difficult. There is also the danger that an improper overthrow will bring great harm to those who are advancing. The evil entity must be openly denounced; the leader of your group must be truthfully told of the plan and so must your associates or comrades in arms. It will benefit you at this time to undertake a project. During this time of overthrow of evil, the superior person will help those

under him with his assets and will render assistance.
Neither will he be content with his yesterday's honors but will press on to ever greater achievements.

Willi believed that the five powerful people who were
going to overthrow Burt were herself, her mother and father,
her therapist, and the judge or perhaps a divorce lawyer if
she hired one. This time she was resolved to follow the counsel of the I Ching exactly.

Burt's trial for beating her was a week away and Willi
wasn't sure about what to do at the trial. She talked to her
mother and father and to her therapist. They all said the same
thing, that Burt had to be punished for the beating he gave
her or he would probably do it again. Willi didn't love Burt
anymore; the beating had knocked that out of her, but she
didn't hate him and didn't really want to see him go to jail.
She felt that he, too, was a victim; in his case the victim of
his father's poor example and advice.

Willi did another reading. Her question was, "What is my
best course of action with regard to Burt's trial?" The answer
was Kua 21, Shih Ho, Corrective Punishment. The text of the
kua reads:

This kua depicts being punished and punishing
others, primarily, but not solely, for criminal offenses. It is favorable to administer justice, which

brings success. The best way to deter wrongdoers is
to make the law absolutely clear and to make punishment swift and certain.

That was certainly clear. There were no moving lines.

Burt hired a lawyer, Mr. Willis, who contacted Willi and
asked her if she would drop the charges against Burt. He said
that if Burt were convicted of assault, he'd probably go to
jail, it would be on his record for the rest of his life, and
any chance he had to become a policeman would be finished.
Willi said she'd think about it and call him back the next day.
Even though her previous reading about what to do regarding Burt's trial had specifically said: "It is always beneficial to administer justice, which brings success. The best
way to deter both wrongdoers and criminals is to make the
law clear and punishment swift and certain," she wanted
to give Burt the benefit of every opportunity, so that night
she did another reading.

Usually, when questions that imply doubt regarding previous readings are asked, or if the same question is asked
twice, the answer appears nonsensical, but in Willi's case she
again received a direct, straightforward answer. Her question was: "What action should I take with regard to drop-
ping the charges against Burt?" The answer was Kua 6, Sung,
Argument, Dispute, Conflict, Adversaries. The kua reads:

You are sincere but are nonetheless entangled in an argument. It is wise to remain so clearheaded and strong that you are always ready to meet your opponent halfway and arrange a settlement. Remaining open to the settling of the argument brings good fortune. To carry the argument to the end brings misfortune. It will be to your advantage to seek guidance from a qualified person and to set out to accomplish a great aim. Make certain your plans are well laid.

Reading that, Willi was ready to meet Burt halfway and drop the charges, but then she read the moving line, 5. Line 5 reads:

To take your argument before a judge, arbiter, or the one in authority brings supreme good fortune.

Willi said that she was stunned by the way the reading told her exactly what to do about her question, even mentioning the judge. That settled the question in Willi's mind.

She called Mr. Willis the next morning and told him that she would not drop the charges. The following week, Willi went to court and testified concerning what had happened. Burt's lawyer made a good case for him and asked for leniency for Burt because it would ruin any chances he had to become a policeman. The judge had a reputation for being hard on offenders who assaulted others. He told Mr. Willis that Burt should have thought about that before he beat his wife. He found Burt guilty of assault and sentenced him to ninety days in jail for assault and ordered him to put himself into a program of therapy for one year following his release. The judge also issued a restraining order against Burt, preventing him from going anywhere near Willi.

Willi made plans to go ahead with her divorce. Because she had been working in a law firm for five years, she thought she could probably handle her own divorce without the expense of a lawyer. She did a reading. Willi's question was: "What can I expect if I conduct my own divorce procedure?" The answer was Kua 40, Hsieh, Abatement of Danger. The text of Kua 40 reads:

> The danger subsides. If there is anything yet to be done to complete the abatement of the danger, it should be attended to immediately so that there will be no reoccurrence. When everything has been attended to, normal actions and conditions should be returned to as quickly as possible. To hasten the process and to complete the abatement, forgive mistakes and pardon even intentional transgressions. Only a superior person acts in that manner.

Willi's answer had a moving line, the bottom line. The bottom line reads:

> The abatement is just beginning. You do not have the strength needed to bring the abatement about, so just remain quiet. The danger will pass of its own accord or with the help of a friend or highly placed associate who will aid you because you did not foolishly try to abate the danger on your own.

Willi was elated that her question had again been answered so accurately. She told me that it was as if she were talking to an incredibly wise grandfather who was actually answering the specific questions she asked. I told her that it was a nice way of thinking about it, and that it was probably very close to the mark.

She wisely resolved not to try and handle her own divorce, but to hire a lawyer. She asked the lawyers in her firm to recommend a good divorce lawyer. They did, and she hired Mr. Grear the next day. Not wanting to make any mistake, she did a reading to see if she had hired the right person. Willi's question was: "What can I expect from using Mr. Grear as the attorney in my divorce suit?" The answer was Kua 34, Ta Chuang, Great Power, Great Strength. The text of Kua 34 reads:

The lower trigram of three solid lines possesses great power, and the lines want to advance. Added to this already great power is the aggressive upward movement of the upper trigram, which is symbolized by thunder. Together, they represent an irresistible force. Knowing that advance is certain, the superior person takes thought to advance correctly. That means advancing virtuously, with good intentions, and only along socially accepted paths. Perseverance in virtue will ensure that when the advance has been accomplished, the superior person will be able to enjoy the results of his advance, rather than being harassed because of the results of an improper advance.

Line 4 was a moving line. The text of line 4 reads:

You are strong and in an excellent position next to those in power. You may move confidently forward, being careful not to use your great strength to excess. All resistance disappears, and for moving ahead virtuously, you suffer no entanglements.

Willi knew she could move confidently ahead with Mr. Grear. Best of all, the kua which Kua 34 turned into by virtue of its moving line was Kua 11, T'ai, Peaceful Prosperity, Harmony. The text of Kua 11 reads:

This kua is formed of the upper trigram of Earth, whose motion is downward, and the lower trigram of Heaven, whose motion is upward. The two come together, forming the condition of Heaven on Earth. The light force is in the ascendancy, and the dark force is diminishing. People in high places are considerate of their subordinates, and subordinates are respectful and helpful to those in power. It is a time when feuds end and friendships renew. Harmony prevails; pettiness ends. People act from their higher natures rather than from their lower. There is perfect correspondence in all areas, meaning that everyone gets along with everyone else. It is a time of good fortune and success, a time when small efforts bring large rewards. This time of harmony can be lengthened by healing dissension, making an extra effort to get along with others, being extra courteous and considerate, and participating in every way that is in accord with this time of Heaven on Earth.

Today, Willi is remarried, has a one year old son, and is expecting a second child in a few months. She married well this time. Her husband is again an auto mechanic, and, from what Willi reports, is a fine husband and a good father in every way.

The Smoker

In 1985 I was leading a series of month-long workshops that dealt with the subject of obtaining and keeping power; power to live one's life as one wishes to live it; power to have what one wants and to be what one wants; power to have the free time to enjoy it all. One of the workshop participants, Mr. Paley, had come from Florida to participate in the workshop. We became quite friendly, and when he learned during the course of the workshop that I was interested in the I Ching, he related the following story to me. I asked his permission to include his story in this collection so that others can benefit from his experience. He agreed, and provided me with his readings as well as those of his daughter, Susanna, with whom I had several informative conversations.

Mr. Paley was a successful businessman in his sixties. He and his wife, Emma, lived in Florida in a beautiful home on a man–made canal. They had three grown children, all married, a dog, a cat, and a boat tied to the back of their house. Mr. Paley was semi-retired, only going into the insurance office he owned once or twice a week. He had been healthy most of his life although he smoked two packs of cigarettes a day, an addiction he had acquired in high school.

Lately, Mr. Paley hadn't been feeling well. He was very nervous and agitated, and he fidgeted a lot. He was also becoming short of temper and several times had snapped at his wife, whom he dearly loved and toward whom he had always been very considerate. He was losing weight, and while he had always had a hearty appetite, now he didn't enjoy his food anymore and didn't have much of an appetite. He exercised regularly, although lately he hadn't enjoyed that either the way he used to, and he had lost his zest for life. He didn't have any bad health habits other than his cigarette smoking.

Mr. Paley's oldest daughter, Susanna, was an I Ching enthusiast. She was worried about her father and asked him to do a reading with her. Mr. Paley had never put much stock in what he called his daughter's "fanciful flights of fortune telling," but he agreed to do the reading. Mr. Paley's question was: "What's wrong with my health?" Susanna showed him how to manipulate the yarrow stalks, and Mr. Paley's answer was Kua 47, K'un, Oppression. The text of Kua 47 reads:

> The onset of adversity, misfortune, and hard times is at hand; all of them can bring about exhaustion and despondency. The superior person takes every turn of events, no matter how dire the events, and out of them creates good fortune. So certain is he

of his ability to turn events into good fortune that he will stake his very life upon his conviction.

There was one moving line, 2. Line 2 reads:

Adversity oppresses you to the point that you cannot even enjoy your meals, and no help is forthcoming from friends or associates. However, a highly placed official is likely to appear, and you may get some assistance from him. Your situation requires you to make a sacrifice now of effort, time, or resources, but the sacrifice will have good results. Do not undertake anything at this time.

Mr. Paley was frightened by the reading; it described his situation so accurately. He asked Susanna what he should do next. She said that the highly placed official who would likely appear was most likely a doctor, and rather than wait for him to appear, her father should go see him.

By virtue of the moving line, Kua 47 turned into Kua 45, Ts'ui, Gathering Together, Joining. The text of Kua 45 reads:

You are called upon either to join a group or gather others into a group. In joining, your motivation should be clear and strong; in gathering a group, your cause must be well-defined, one around

which everyone can gather and which all will support. To achieve a successful end, seek advice from
a qualified person before beginning. Do not slacken
until your objective is reached. You will be called
upon to make sacrifices to obtain your goal. Making
sacrifices is appropriate. Success will be yours.

Mr. Paley asked his daughter what the group was. She
said she didn't know, but it would be revealed to him.

He went to see his doctor for a check-up. The doctor
couldn't find anything obviously wrong with him but told
him, as he had many times in the past, that he must give
up smoking. Mr. Paley said he had tried to quit on a great
number of occasions, but it was too stressful. "Besides," he
said, "I like to smoke."

The doctor said, "Mr. Paley, I've been your doctor for
ten years. I don't know what is wrong with you; you don't
have any cancer I can detect, but I'll wager your lungs are
black with tar and nicotine and they're not delivering the
oxygen you need for optimum health. It's true that we can
live on half of one lung, but not well. Simply stated, I believe
you're not getting enough air. Let's make a little test." The
doctor placed an oxygen tube in Mr. Paley's mouth. He
breathed in the oxygen, and in a few minutes was feeling better and said so. "Of course," said the doctor, "breathing in
richer oxygen will make anyone feel better, but I think in

your case, it's an indication that the problem is what I've said it is."

"Oh, God, Doc," said Mr. Paley, "I've tried to quit lots of times, I just wasn't able to do it, and it darn near drove me out of my mind. I wasn't fit to live with."

The doctor said, "I recommend that you join a group here in town that helps smokers quit. They have an excellent success record and will lend you the support you need to be able to quit. You probably even know some of the people who belong to the group."

Mr. Paley was amazed when he heard the doctor's words. This was certainly the group the reading had referred to. He agreed to join. Later that night he called his daughter and told her about his meeting with the doctor. She was excited for him and pleased that the reading had been so accurate. Mr. Paley asked if he could do another reading. She told him to come right over.

The next question Mr. Paley asked was: "What can I expect as a result of joining the stop-smoking group?" His answer was Kua 52, Kên, Mountain, Stopping Action, Thoughts Coming to Rest. The text of 52 reads:

Universal law provides for the alternation of movement and rest, each at its proper time. If you remain still when the time for action is at hand, you will miss your opportunity, and what would have been easy becomes difficult. If you are in action when the time for rest is at hand, you will be unprepared when the time for action comes. When actions stop and thoughts come to rest, the sanest person achieves a quiet heart.

Susanna told her father that it was a very good response, that Ken, Mountain, meant "stopping," and that it almost certainly meant that by joining the group he would be able to quit. He asked her if it might not mean that he should stop himself from joining the group. Susanna said it would have meant that if his question had been, "What action should I take regarding my joining the stop-smoking group?" but since his question was, "What can I expect as a result of joining the stop-smoking group?" the answer meant that he would be able to stop smoking. Susanna told him that it was also possible that the reading meant that he would quit the group after joining, but that she didn't think that was what it meant.

There were two moving lines in the answer, 4 and 6. The text of Line 4 reads:

You are nearing the attainment of your goals, but are still agitated. Practice achieving calmness. Learn to operate from deep inner levels and learn to restrain your egotistical drive.

Susanna told her father that she thought it would benefit him greatly if he learned to meditate, that it was a wonderful way of calming oneself. He asked what the purpose of meditation was. Susanna told him that it was way of clearing the mind of thoughts, to quiet the mind so that information of a divine nature could come in. He agreed to give it a try.

The text of Line 6 reads:

By maintaining a quiet state of mind and not acting rashly, you will be successful.

That seemed to reinforce Susanna's suggestion that he learn meditation and it also promised success. The kua that Kua 52 turned into by virtue of its moving lines was Kua 62, Hsiao Kuo, Attention to Detail, and Small Tasks, Avoiding Excesses. The text of Kua 62 reads:

This is a time when great good fortune may be obtained by paying strict attention to minor details, attempting only the achievement of lesser goals, and avoiding excessive behavior. In expenditures, be thrifty but avoid miserliness; in bereavement, be truly sorrowful but avoid outward displays meant to impress others; in conduct be modest but avoid groveling.

Susanna said that she thought it meant that he would be very successful provided that he paid attention to even the smallest details of what the people in his new group would teach him. And learning to meditate would help.

Mr. Paley wanted to ask another question. It was: "What can I expect with regard to my health as a result of stopping smoking?" His answer was Kua 24, Fu, Return of the Light Force. The text of Kua 24 reads:

> The forces of light and darkness constantly fluctuate, the increase of one showing a decrease of the other. No matter how careful one is, there are always digressions from the path of the superior person. What is important is that one turn back before going too far. The ancient text of this kua says, "the way goes backwards and forwards; on the seventh day comes return." The text indicates that success is forthcoming, that friends come without blame, and that having somewhere to go or something to do will enhance your position.

There was a moving line, 5, which reads:

> You are in a commanding position but have strayed from the path of the superior person. Because of your inner resolve to be the best that you can be,

you turn back to the good path, having resolved not to stray from it again. For your prompt action in returning to the path of the superior person, you will never be sorry for having strayed from the path or for returning to it.

Mr. Paley was pleased with the reading, which clearly depicted his situation and promised that he would not be sorry for having returned to the path of good health.

Because of the moving line, Kua 24 became Kua 3, Chun, Difficulty and Danger at the Beginning. The text of Kua 3 reads:

In the beginning of all things, great care must be taken if planting is to lead to harvesting. In the beginning, everything necessary for complete fulfillment is present but not in its proper place; there exists a state of confusion. Therefore, no immediate action should be taken. You should wait, and during the waiting, you should obtain helpers.

Proceeding in this manner, the superior person brings order out of confusion and works supreme success.

Mr. Paley was eager to begin his new program of health. He consulted with his doctor again, met with the group and joined. Mr. Paley said that at first he was reluctant to tell anyone that he had quit smoking, but that after six months, he was confident that he had put smoking into his past forever. His urge to smoke had gone, and he had a great number of new friends. Today, Mr. Paley is the leader of the group, and he has brought in many new members.

Hurrah for Mr. Paley! Hurrah for Susanna! With Susanna's help, he turned back onto the path of the superior person, for which we can all rejoice.

Winning Her Man

Kirsten, twenty-five years old, was in love with Stephan who was four years older. She hoped to marry him in the near future. The problem was his mother, Elsa. She was the head of the household since Stephan's father had died four years before, and she didn't believe Kirsten was good enough for her son. She always tried to discourage Stephan from dating Kirsten, and never invited Kirsten to their family affairs, which were frequent.

Kirsten was an intelligent girl and had many fine qualities. She was loyal, trustworthy, kind, compassionate, a good cook, and fun to be with. Her father who had learned how to use the I Ching from me when Kirsten was only five years old had taught her how to use it. Kirsten did a reading to see what she should do to accomplish her goal of marrying Stephan. Her answer was Kua 36, Persecution.

> A weak, petty adversary, that could be either a person or a group, is bent on harming, persecuting, or victimizing you. Many possible motives, such as resentment,

jealousy, the adversary's belief that he or she is protecting another, or sheer malice, may exist. Perhaps your adversary may fear that you will undermine their status or resources, or establish a relationship with someone he or she may not want you to have a relationship with, or accomplish something that they see as potentially damaging or detrimental. Their persecution is an attempt to undermine you and weaken your position so you will not be able to accomplish what they fear. If you are to maintain your position and succeed in attaining your goal during this time of adversity, persevere in what you know to be right, and behave with the utmost discretion in every way. Most importantly, avoid calling attention to your wealth, resources, ability and intelligence, or you will risk antagonizing the adversary further. Continue to follow the path of honor and integrity, and act always from your higher nature rather than your lower. Be modest and unassuming. Avoid claiming credit for your accomplishments, but share your credit with others. Do not abandon your goal unless you believe that you might cause irreparable harm to yourself or to others if you persist. The best way to guarantee your success in this situation is to bide your time; to go about your affairs with the utmost discretion and caution; and to avoid any forceful, aggressive, or extreme behaviors or actions that could arouse resentment or resistance. Be content with any minor gains you can make while remaining inwardly perservering in reaching your goal.

It was obvious from the reading that Elsa was a threat to Kirsten's plan to marry Stephan and was doing what she could to undermine the relationship. Kirsten decided to lie low, not attend the family affairs, not call Stephan while he was at home, only talk with him on his cell phone when he was away from home, and not take up too much of his time. The moving line was the bottom line.

You are strong and just starting out. You want to press forward quickly but are confused and uncertain about the correct path to follow. If you live in a state of perpetual hurry, you will never attain composure, and stress will exhaust you. Composure is a state in which the mind is settled, calm, and tranquil. If you can attain that state, you will be able to act without stress, and will, therefore, make no mistakes. Take your time. Be patient. Do not let yourself be steered off your course by outside influences, but remain steadfast in your determination to reach your goal. During this time of new beginnings, the first actions you take will determine the success or failure of what is to come later. Remember that character is the bowstring from which we shoot the arrows of the future. We must renew our efforts each day to shape our character, for nothing else is as important to our life and success. Proceed with great reverence in your heart for All-That-Is and remain steadfast in your intent to reach your goal in the right way.

The bottom line suggests that she should go away for a short period of time and let her absence speak for itself. The line also suggested a short period of fasting to clarify her mind.

Kirsten was a real estate agent and was the number one agent in the county in which she lived. She had saved a good deal of money and had invested it wisely in the real estate market. She could easily afford to follow the advice in the bottom line and go away for a couple of weeks. She chose a health resort in Mexico where they specialized in fasting and cleansing diets. She informed Stephan of her decision, saying she needed a break from work, and left a week later. She informed Stephan there was no cell phone reception where she was going, but that she would call him every few days.

Kirsten was massaged, put on a special cleansing diet, hot tubbed, steamed, and she swam in the pool and relaxed completely. She called Stephan at the end of the week and he said he missed her terribly. She did not mention his mother or their relationship, but said she was relaxing and doing a lot of soul searching. Stephan became immediately concerned and asked if she was having second thoughts about their relationship. Kirsten said that she loved Stephan very much, but said that her idea of marriage was where both families wholeheartedly embraced the son or daughter's choice. She said she didn't think it possible for them to ever have a real marriage, one in which their children would have an extended family relationship because Elsa didn't approve of her for Stephan's wife. Stephan said she would be marrying him, not his mother. Kirsten said that was not completely true, that he had a close relationship with his mother that would hopefully continue after they were married. She told him to think about it and she would talk further with him when she came home.

Kirsten did a reading at the end of her second week at the spa. Her question was, "What action should I take regarding marrying Stephan?" Her answer was Kua 10.

This kua depicts you "treading on the tail of a tiger," meaning a powerful person or group who can cause you harm. However, even though you tread on the tiger's tail, it will not bite you because you are sincere and agreeable and know how to behave properly.

Such behavior brings you success. The key to your success lies in cultivating a pleasing and sincere personality, which will bring you success and good fortune because the person or group represented by the tiger will trust and respect you. Pleasant manners win over even bad-tempered people. If you do not let their unpleasantness irritate or upset you, your own pleasant manners will have a positive and calming effect on them. Receiving this kua as your answer foretells that you will have success if you accept the guidance of this kua.

It was clear to her that she needed to confront Stephan's mother. She knew from her reading that if she behaved correctly, she would be successful in winning her over. The moving line, 4 reads:

You are strong and in a position of trust. The situation calls for you to move forward, but doing so may entail a dangerous confrontation with a powerful person. There is danger in the confrontation. This situation calls for great care and caution, but, if you proceed carefully, you will find good fortune. Friendly, good-natured, polite conduct will benefit you greatly. Hold your goal firmly in your mind, remain persevering but cautious, and you will achieve your goal.

Line 4 assured her she would win through to her goal of marrying Stephan with his mother's blessing if she conducted herself properly.

The resultant kua was Kua 61: Emptiness, Openness.

In this kua, two broken lines in the center of four solid lines represent emptiness. This is a time for you to be clear about your goals and about making decisions regarding others. The way in which you can achieve that clarity is by emptying your mind of all prejudiced thoughts, foregone conclusions, or conscious expectations. Let your mind be open, receptive, and free of preconceived ideas. Once you achieve that state of emptiness, you will be open to receiving wisdom and knowledge from other sources such as people, objects, books, and the Universe itself. It will be as if you have opened your pure mind—the mind you were born with—and are welcoming in information, knowledge, and wisdom. That openness will make it possible for you to perceive the state of mind of others. Your understanding of them will increase, and your ability to inspire them to follow you and to do your bidding will increase.

If you cultivate open-mindedness, you will earn the respect of all around you. You will also often find solutions that might otherwise escape you, and you will seldom make errors of judgment. Because you have opened your mind to vast sources of knowledge and information, you will speak words of such great wisdom that you will influence not only all those around you but also, as the ancient text states, "the pigs and fishes," which is a comical way of saying that you will influence even those who are hard to influence.

Practicing the pursuit of emptiness will bring you good fortune, and your perceptions will bloom like flowers during a perfect summer. Your inner clarity will make it possible for you to discuss difficult problems and to resolve them. You will benefit from undertaking a major project at this time, and it will bring you good fortune.

Kirsten determined that she would not hold any preconceived ideas about Elsa or the relationship, and that she would just remain open. Upon her return home she called Elsa and said she was prepared to discontinue her relationship with Stephan but that she wanted to have one final meeting with Elsa before she did that. Surprisingly, Elsa agreed. They met the next day for lunch. Kirsten told Elsa about her belief that a marriage should involve the entire family. She said she had misgivings about Elsa being willing to do that. She said that Stephan loved his mother, and she wanted that to continue, but she believed that unless Elsa could accept her for a daughter-in-law, her relationship with Stephan would be hurt and their marriage would suffer. She said that making a marriage work was difficult under even the best of circumstances and to have it start off under circumstances that were less than good was just putting too much at risk.

She went on to say that she believed that because Stephan loved her, if she gave him up because his mother couldn't accept her as his wife, that he would resent that, perhaps for many years.

Elsa listened carefully to everything that Kirsten said and thanked her kindly. Kirsten asked Elsa why she believed she was not right for her son. Elsa said she didn't know Kirsten that well and was just going on her instinct. Kirsten suggested they talk for a while, not about each other, but about life in general. Kirsten relied heavily on the wisdom she had learned from using the *I Ching*. They talked for two hours. At the end of the conversation, Elsa said she would think about it overnight and get back to her the next day. Kirsten said that would be fine. They hugged each other and each went on her way.

Kirsten did a reading that night about what she could expect from the meeting. Her answer was Kua 37.

This kua indicates an influence now or soon to come in your life that has to do with a family or group of

which you are or will be a part. Being part of a family or group will enable you to accomplish much more than you can alone and will bring you good fortune. Keep in mind that you should conduct yourself as a person of honor and integrity at all times, not just with members of your family or group, but with everyone. Such behavior will bring honor to your family or group and will also earn you their honor and respect, which is a great credit to you, and one that you should work diligently to obtain. You can achieve that respect by living up to the model of the superior person in every way. Superior people live up to their word, meaning that they do what they say they will do and they always speak the truth. Also, their words and actions are always in harmony, and, if they say that being trustworthy is important, they should always be trustworthy. This kua depicts the inner structure and dynamics of a family or group. When all members fulfill their respective duties and show the appropriate love and respect to one another, the family or group functions efficiently and harmoniously. Families and groups should establish common traditions and beliefs, meaning that they should agree to continue to uphold honorable principles in common, rather than adopting every passing trend, and that they are loyal and dedicated to all the other members. Internal conflict or dissension weakens the power of families and groups to act as a unit in overcoming external dangers.

Kirsten went to sleep with a smile on her face. The next day she received a call from Elsa saying she had a long talk with Stephan that morning and she was calling to wish her and Stephan a wonderful life together. Kirsten was elated, but still cautious. She got out her *I Ching* and did another reading asking, "What can I expect being married to Stephan?" Her answer was Kua 40, Abatement of Danger.

The danger subsides. If your question concerns the taking of action, taking that action will cause the danger to completely dissipate, thus bringing you good fortune. Reflect carefully on the entire situation related to your question. If you need to take any further steps to finish abating the danger, attend to those immediately so that there will be no chance of it recurring. Avoid spending too much time deliberating. Once you have considered any matter carefully, anxious hesitation will only cause you to miss your opportunity, for too much reflection cripples the power of decision. After you have reduced or eliminated the danger, return to your normal actions and conditions as quickly as possible. Only take whatever actions are necessary to reduce or eliminate the danger. To reduce or eliminate the danger that threatens, resolve any open conflicts, settle any existing arguments, forgive mistakes, and pardon even intentional violations. Such actions will lessen any remaining tensions and pave the way for a return to normal conditions. After the danger has completely subsided, you may feel so relieved that you want to celebrate. That is natural, but avoid letting yourself be carried away, for that will work against you. By quickly taking the actions necessary to abate the danger, you will have good fortune.

The moving line was the bottom line.

The danger is beginning to lessen and will soon be gone. The only action you should take is to continue on the path to achieving your goal and make certain that your actions are in accord with the highest standards of integrity. If you persevere on that path, the danger will subside completely, and you will achieve success and meet your goal.

Kirsten was elated. She knew that she still had to be cautious around Elsa, but she knew her relationship with Stephan would be off to a good start. The result was Kua 54, Entrance Into or Maintaining a Relationship.

This kua depicts you in a difficult and unbalanced situation where you are either in a relationship or about to enter into a relationship of some kind. It could be a personal or love relationship, a partnership, a company, organization, a family, or any other type of group. In all cases, the situation is unfavorable because weak people have strong positions of influence and feel threatened by you. With regard to a personal or love relationship, maintaining it or entering into it requires that you be modest and gentle because aggressiveness on your part will arouse resentment and resistance either from the person with whom you want to have the relationship or those close to that person. Those close to the person will try to undermine you, either to protect the person from you or to protect their own relationship with that person. With regard to a group to which you already belong or which you would like to join, aggressiveness on your part will arouse resentment and resistance from some members. You must be able to fit yourself in smoothly without arousing anger, suspicion, fear, or distrust. Those already in the group are possessive of their positions and influence, and if you threaten them in any way, it will work to your disadvantage.

Relationships that are legally formed have a contract as a basis for conduct, but relationships based on voluntary participation require great tact and thoughtfulness if you are to successfully maintain or integrate yourself into the relationship or group. To be successful in your endeavor, you must exercise great caution, be willing to do more than your share, remain exceptionally modest, unobtrusive, friendly, open, and inviting, downplay your talent, good looks, and assets, and be careful not to threaten anyone's position. In that way, you will have the best chance of attaining your goal. However, it is a difficult situation. Neither good fortune nor misfortune is indicated by this kua because your success is entirely dependent on how you conduct yourself and how the members or the person receives you.

When Kirsten read it, her enthusiasm dampened a bit because she knew she would have to continue to be extremely careful around Elsa, but she also knew she could do that. She and Stephan were married that fall. It was a beautiful wedding.

part three
A BRIEF HISTORY
OF THE I CHING

CHAPTER SIX

A Brief History of the I Ching

Thousands of years ago, before the dawn of written history, legend has it that there lived a great Chinese sage known as Fu Hsi. It is said that he was the man who first united all of China, becoming her first emperor. He is also credited with leading the Chinese people from the age of hunting and fishing into the age of agriculture. (For the complete story of how this author believes Fu Hsi originated the I Ching system, chose his first disciple, and sent the wisdom on its way to us through the long chain of ages, read, *A Tale of The I Ching.*)

A man of incredibly vast intellect, Fu Hsi, over a period of time and in stages, conceived of a mathematical model of the Universe, complete with all its conditions and elements of change, the sixty-four six-line figures.

Legend has it that in forming the sixty-four kua of the I Ching, Fu Hsi surveyed the vast diversities and movements under Heaven, saw the ways the movements met and became interrelated, saw the ways their courses were governed by eternal laws. He thought through the order of the outer world to its end and explored his own nature to its deepest core. He perceived the beginning of all things that lay unmoving, in the beyond, in the form of ideas that have yet to manifest themselves. He put himself in accord with those ideas and, in so doing, arrived at an understanding of fate.

Writing did not exist at the time of Fu Hsi, so his teachings were handed down in the oral tradition, one generation faithfully teaching another, perhaps for a thousand years or more. When writing began in China five thousand years ago, about the year 3,000 B.C., the I Ching teachings and the answers to questions were first inscribed on bones, some of which have been discovered and preserved. They are called *oracle bones*.

Two thousand more years passed, during which time the I Ching and its teachings flourished. In the twelfth century B.C., the tyrant, Chou Shin, ruled. He was to be the last emperor of the Shang Dynasty (1766–1121 B.C.). He was a cruel and heartless man who tortured people to pleasure himself and his equally cruel and sadistic concubine. So cruel was he that all of China lived in fear of him.

At the same time there also lived a man named Wen, a learned I Ching scholar of rare insight, who governed a small province in a remote area of western China. Wen governed his people according to I Ching principles and was, therefore, as much loved and respected by the people as Chou Shin was hated and feared.

It is written that one day an army came to invade Wen's little domain, but when they saw how orderly it was, how prosperous were its citizens, how peaceful and harmoniously they lived together, the leaders sent their army home and stayed to study with Wen.

The people urged Wen to gather an army and overthrow the tyrant, Chou Shin, assuring him that they would willingly follow him. Wen replied that since he was truly a law-abiding citizen, he could not in good conscience take action against the emperor.

Chou Shin heard the rumors that Wen was being asked to gather an army to rise against him and had Wen arrested and put into prison. Wen was allowed to live, but only because of his great popularity.

During the year 1143 B.C., the year that Wen was in confinement and in fear for his life, he used the I Ching's great wisdom and its divinatory powers to keep himself alive. In Wen's time, there were two versions of the I Ching: Gai Tsung and Lien San, and during his time of isolation, he reinterpreted the names of the kua and other portions of the great books. He also changed the order of the kua established by Fu Hsi to the order currently in use in every known version of the I Ching. The order in which the kua appear does not in any way affect the readings.

In 1122 B.C., Wen's oldest son, Yu, after publicly denouncing Emperor Chou Shin to turn public opinion hotly against him, gathered an army and overthrew the tyrant and became king. The new king, to honor his father, bestowed upon him the title of "King," and Wen was forever after known as King Wen, even though he never ruled as king. King Yu died a few years after becoming king, leaving his thirteen year old son as heir to the throne. The inexperienced youngster was incapable of ruling, so King Wen's younger son, Tan, known as the Duke of Chou, ruled in his stead. King Wen had instructed Tan in the teachings of the I Ching, and it was Tan who, during his reign as acting king, interpreted the meanings of the 384 individual lines of the kua. The I Ching was then considered complete. The year was 1109 B.C.

So profound was the wisdom of King Wen and his sons, wisdom that had been passed on to them by their ancestors and increased by their own study of the I Ching, that they were able to provide a foundation for their dynasty so strong that it lasted for 800 years, the longest in the history of China.

Several hundred more years passed, and in 551 B.C., the great sage and scholar, Confucius, came onto the world scene. In his later years he began the study of the I Ching, and when he was past the age of seventy he humorously commented, "If some years were added to my life, I would give fifty to the study of the I Ching, and might then escape from falling into great error."

Confucius wrote many commentaries to the *Book of Changes*, most of which are reproduced in other versions of the I Ching, notably, that wonderful version published by Princeton University Press, Bollingen Series XIX, the Wilhelm/Baynes translation. Should you become so engaged with the I Ching that you wish to go beyond using it as an oracle and begin studying it as a book of wisdom, you will surely want to obtain that most thorough and profound work.

CHARACTERISTICS OF THE LINES

Generally speaking, the characteristics of the solid and the broken lines are as follows:

SOLID	BROKEN
Strong	Weak
Virtuous	Evil
Light-giving	Dark
Aggressive	Gentle

The characteristics of either kind of line can be modified by the meaning of the kua, but such modifications will always be stated in the kua.

CORRECTNESS

Before a kua is formed, there are six empty places that the lines will fill. Three of the six places require strong lines, meaning solid lines, and three of the places require weak lines, meaning broken lines. The places 1, 3, and 5 are strong and require strong, solid lines. These lines are then considered correct because they are strong lines in strong places. Places 2, 4, and 6 require weak, broken lines. These lines are then considered correct because they are weak lines in weak places. When a weak line is in a place which calls for a strong line, it is generally unequal to the task at hand. When a strong line is in a place which calls for a weak line, it is generally too aggressive for the task at hand. Keep in mind that those are general rules and can be modified according to special conditions of the kua, but any such special conditions will always be stated in the kua.

CORRESPONDENCE

Each of the lines corresponds to one other line. The bottom line of the lower trigram, Line 1, corresponds to the bottom line of the upper trigram, Line 4. Similarly, the middle line of the lower trigram, Line 2, corresponds to the middle line

of the upper trigram, Line 5. The top line of the lower trigram, Line 3, corresponds to the top line of the upper trigram, Line 6.

When corresponding lines are the same, both broken
or both solid, they generally oppose each other as do the
positive ends of two magnets facing each other: the force of
one repels the force of the other.

When corresponding lines are different, they are helpful to each other. For instance, when a strong ruler, who will
be represented by an solid line in the fifth place, has a com-
pliant official, who will be represented by a broken line in
the second place, there is no conflict, and the official carries out his ruler's orders. If the ruler is weak, a broken line
in the fifth place, and the official strong, a solid line in the
second place, the ruler can still rely on his trustworthy official to carry out his orders. If the ruler is strong and the
official is strong, unbroken lines in the second and fifth
places, the chances are that the official will be headstrong,
argumentative, and insubordinate, arguing with his ruler—
not a good condition. If the ruler and the official are both
weak, broken lines in the second and fifth places, they will
not be strong enough to make progress. Remember that
these are general rules and can be overridden by a particular situation or condition of the kua. Such conditions or
situations will be detailed in the kua.

CONDITION

Line 1, the bottom line, indicates the onset of the condition depicted in the kua. It will soon manifest itself or has just barely begun to manifest itself.

Line 2 shows the condition having manifested and growing stronger, but because of the favorableness of the line in the middle of the lower trigram, the condition is usually under control.

Line 3 is at the top of the lower trigram, so the condition has grown stronger than in Line 2 and is usually unstable because, as all the lines enter the kua from the bottom and move upward through the six stages of change, Line 3 is about to leave the lower trigram and move into the upper trigram. That is almost always a somewhat dangerous transition because to get from the lower trigram to the upper, one must make a leap. In a life situation, it would be similar to quitting one's job before another job had been obtained. The period in between jobs could be dangerous. When a rabbit runs from one bit of cover to another; in the middle, he is vulnerable.

Line 4 shows the condition approaching its maximum potential; therefore, depending on whether the condition bodes good or evil, one must be cautious. Additional caution is required because Line 4 is next to Line 5, which is usually the ruler. Being close to a ruler can be very good, but it can also be very dangerous. If the situation warrants it, the kua will state which condition prevails.

Line 5 shows the condition having reached its maximum potential. Any movement beyond that point will cause the condition to turn toward its opposite: fullness to emptiness, increase to decrease, abundance to want, safety to danger.

Line 6, the top line, shows the condition depicted in the kua having exceeded its maximum potential and consequently turning toward its opposite condition.

POSITION

The bottom line can represent a newcomer, someone just about to join a group, or a subordinate in the lowest position. He will generally not have any title or influence.

Line 2 occupies the center of the lower trigram and indicates that the person it represents is in a position of minor leadership. He has some authority, and in an organization may have a minor title. In the army, he would be perhaps a lieutenant or a sergeant, not a general. Being in the center of the lower trigram, he will have some influence with his peers or associates, and he will have a relationship with the leader, Line 5.

Line 3 is the top line of the lower trigram and represents a person who is rising in the ranks. He has attained some stature and is about to advance to the upper trigram, a somewhat dangerous move. The danger in the move is caused by the necessity of leaving his position in the lower trigram and "jumping" into the upper trigram. The time between jumping and landing is dangerous.

Line 4 is next to the ruler, which can be fortunate, or it can be dangerous, or both, depending on the circumstances. The person who is the subject of Line 4 is considered to be the ruler's minister, an able general, or a strong vice president. He is usually in a position of trust. It is almost always beneficial for the ruler and the minister to be represented by lines of a different character, meaning broken and solid lines, for that means that they will not be in conflict.

Line 5 occupies the center of the upper trigram, which is generally the position of the ruler. This line usually controls the kua. It is almost always beneficial if this line is the opposite of Lines 2 and 4 so that conflict is avoided. When it is beneficial for the lines not to be opposite, the kua will so state.

The top line in ancient times represented a great sage who had left the affairs of the world behind him but who could be called upon in any great emergency. Today, it might represent a person who has served his country or his organization well and has retired and retreated from worldly affairs, but who still has influence. It could be a wise grandfather who was the head of his family for many years who is now old and somewhat inactive, but can be called upon for advice and leadership in times of need.

TIME

Each line represents a time earlier or later in the kua according to its position. The bottom line represents the earliest time and the top line the latest time. Only the four middle lines represent the time that is active within the situation. Lines 1 and 6 represent the time just before and just after the active time.

HOLDING TOGETHER

Lines next to each other hold together if they are different and do not hold together if they are the same. The most important of these relationships is that of the fourth and fifth lines, the ruler and his minister, and the best condition for those two lines occurs when the ruler is strong and the minister weak. The line above is said to "rest" on the line below, and the line below is said to "receive" from the line above.

If a broken line "rests" on a solid line below, the broken line is well supported. If a solid line "rests" on a broken line, the support is weak. If a broken line "receives" from a solid line above, the broken line is benefited because of the strength of the solid line. If a solid line "receives" from a broken line, the solid line is not usually benefited because of the weakness of the broken line. That is a general rule; any departure from the rule will be stated in the kua.

THE RULERS OF
THE KUA

There are two kinds of rulers: governing and constituting. The governing ruler is generally good and virtuous and is ruler by virtue of position and time. Line 5 is usually the governing ruler, but sometimes another line is the ruler because of the time and the situation.

The constituting ruler is the line that gives the kua its meaning. An example of a constituting ruler giving meaning to a kua can be seen in Kua 9, Hsiao Ch'u, The Restraining Power of the Small. The fourth line, the constituting ruler, represents the weak force that is restraining the other strong lines. The governing ruler of the kua is the strong solid line in the fifth place.

When the governing ruler and the constituting ruler are the same, there is only one ruler, and he is always of good character and holds his position because it is the correct position for him at that time. When the governing ruler and the constituting rulers are different, there are two rulers. In each kua, the governing ruler is indicated by a circle ○ and the constituting ruler by a square □. When they are the same, only a circle is used.

KUA 9

Keep in mind that all of the above comments reflect the general rules but that any rule can be modified within a particular kua. The modification will always be clearly indicated.

THE TRIGRAMS

On the following pages are listed the eight primary trigrams along with their attributes or the objects they represent. The attributes of the trigrams are not inherent in the objects they represent. For instance, the kua of Ch'ien represents: Heaven; the father; and males. Ch'ien's attributes are: creative, strong, and virtuous. That does not mean that all males are creative, strong, and virtuous. In the trigram Kuai, which represents Overthrow of Evil, the person represented by the broken top line of the kua could be either an evil man or an evil woman, depending on the circumstances surrounding your question. It could also be an evil habit or an evil group or an evil characteristic.

THE EIGHT TRIGRAMS AND THEIR ATTRIBUTES

CH'IEN
THE CREATIVE

Heaven, God, strong, male, light-giving, virtuous, good, direct, aggressive, forceful, rigid, unyielding. It is the element that stimulates K'un to bring forth All-That-Is. It is the original, ultimate source. (The motion of the trigram is upward.)

K'UN
THE RECEPTIVE

Earth, mother, female yielding, receptive, gentle, devoted, hollow. It is the element through which Ch'ien brings into being All-That-Is. K'un is the Receptive in that it purely receives, without resistance, all that Ch'ien commands. (The motion of the trigram is downward.)

NOTE: Neither Ch'ien nor K'un is greater than the other, nor are they opposites. They work together to bring into being All-That-Is. Neither one can bring things into a state of being without the help of the other.

CHÊN
AROUSING

Thunder, the force that excites to action, the oldest son, development, forceful. (The motion of the trigram is upward.)

SUN
WIND, WOOD

Penetrating, oldest daughter, gentle, adaptive, a tree, influence. (The motion of the trigram is downward.)

K'AN
WATER, THE ABYSS

Danger, rain, middle son, blood, fear, moon, dark, winter, work, a pit, as in a deep hole. (The motion of the trigram is downward.)

LI
FIRE

Light, reason, clarity, middle daughter, flying bird, flame, cow, weapons. It clings to that which nourishes it as flame to wood or grass to earth. (The motion of the trigram is upward.)

KÊN
MOUNTAIN

Stopping, heavy, youngest son, unmoving, calm, a gate or a door, pausing, inner reserve. (The motion of the trigram is downward.)

T'UI
MARSH, LAKE

Joyous, reservoir, marsh, youngest daughter, gaiety, mouth, magician, pleasure, to break in pieces or to break apart. (The motion of the trigram is upward.)

INNER AND
OUTER TRIGRAMS

The upper trigram is said to be the outer trigram; the lower trigram is said to be the inner trigram.

An example of how the inner and outer trigrams give meaning to the kua can be seen in Kua 15, Ch'ien, "Modesty." The lower trigram is Kên, which means mountain, and the upper trigram is K'un, or Earth (☷). The meaning is therefore a mountain hidden within the Earth, or the image of modesty.

KUA 15

Another example is Kua 29, K'an, "Danger." When the lower trigram is the trigram K'an, the danger exists within the situation. When upper trigram is the trigram K'an, the danger is coming from outside the situation.

KUA 29

NUCLEAR
TRIGRAMS

Each kua contains two "nuclear" trigrams. They are called *nuclear* because they are made up of Lines 2, 3, 4, and 5, or the middle four lines of the kua.

The nuclear trigrams influence the meaning of the individual lines more than they influence the overall meaning of the kua.

The lower nuclear trigram is formed from Lines 2, 3, and 4. The upper nuclear trigram is formed from Lines 3, 4, and 5. Lines 1 and 6 are not affected by the nuclear trigrams because they are not part of either of them.

Line 2 of the kua is part of two trigrams: the lower primary trigram, of which it is the center line, and the lower nuclear trigram, of which it is the bottom line.

Line 3 is part of three trigrams: the lower primary trigram, of which it is the top line, the lower nuclear trigram, of which it is the center line, and the upper nuclear trigram, of which it is the bottom line.

Line 4 is also part of three trigrams: the lower nuclear trigram, of which it is the top line, the upper nuclear trigram, of which it is the middle line, and the upper primary trigram, of which it is the bottom line.

Line 5, like Line 2, is part of two trigrams: the upper nuclear trigram, of which it forms the top line, and the upper primary trigram, of which it forms the middle line.

If a particular line has meaning for you, that is, if it is a moving line and the line is either number 2, 3, 4, or 5, the line will be subtly influenced by the nuclear trigram or trigrams of which it is a part. What the specific influence is will be determined by the nature of the nuclear trigram itself. For instance, if the nuclear trigram is danger, there will be a hint of danger in the situation, and the counsel of the moving line may add a word of caution.

HEAVEN, EARTH, AND MAN

Starting at the bottom of the kua, the first two lines represent Earth, the middle two lines represent Man, and the top two lines represent Heaven. Man in the middle is the entity through which Heaven and Earth interact.

THE MEANING OF THE KUA

The meaning of each kua is generally derived from the attributes of the two trigrams from which it is formed. For example, the meaning of Kua 11, T'ai, is Peaceful Prosperity and Harmony. It is comprised of the trigram of Ch'ien (☰), which represents heaven, and K'un, (☷) which represents

Earth. Earth is over Heaven. The tendency of Earth is to sink, and the tendency of Heaven is to rise; therefore, the two come together bringing about a time of "Heaven on Earth" or Peaceful Prosperity and Harmony.

KUA 11

Sometimes the names and the meanings of the kua are taken from what the six-line figure looks like, as in Kua 50, Ting, The Cauldron, which re-sembles a big pot. The broken bottom line repre-sents the legs; the next three solid lines represent the belly of the pot; the next broken line, the rings or handles by which the cauldron is carried; and the top solid line, the lid.

KUA 50

Some of the kua take their meaning from the action of the lines, as in that of Kua 43, which means Overthrow of Evil. Each of the five lower solid lines represents a strong and virtuous person who has banded with the others to move upward to over-throw the top line, which, being broken, represents, an evil person, a bad habit, an evil group, or any dark force.

KUA 43

CHAPTER SEVEN

The Order of the Kua

The original order of the kua established by Fu Hsi remained in use for two thousand years or more. King Wen changed the order of the kua while in prison in 1143 B.C. He believed that while Fu Hsi's order perfectly represented the larger body of the Universe, it was inappropriate when applied to the everyday affairs of humankind. King Wen's order is now in use in every known version of the *I Ching*.

When I was writing my interpretation of the *I Ching*, I considered changing the order of the kua from the one established by King Wen back to the one originally established by Fu Hsi. I would not make such a change without Universal guidance, so I made an inquiry. I wondered how to phrase the question. There is no answer in the *I Ching* that says, "The correct order of the kua is the Fu Hsi order," or, "The correct order of the kua is the King Wen order." I thought about the problem for several days, and then hit upon the solution. I spoke aloud to All-That-Is, which is how I refer to the Universe and all it contains, and said, "I do not know how to phrase the question about which order to use, but I know that you know what I want to know and how to provide the answer, so I'll proceed on that basis." At the top of my divination page I wrote, "What should I do regarding the order of the kua for the new *I Ching*?" I burned some incense, passed all the articles of divination through the smoke three times, held the thought of what I wanted to know clearly in my mind, and manipulated the yarrow stalks. The resulting numbers for the first line were 3-3-3, a 9, resulting in a solid line that would change into a broken line in the next kua.

Having done this for many years, I sometimes become aware of the answer to a question after seeing only the first or second lines. Manipulating the yarrow stalks and seeing those first lines seems to trigger a response within me, and I perceive what the answer will be. However, even when I think I know the answer, I always finish the manipulation process because many times I find that what I thought was going to be the answer was not.

In the case of my seeing the first line of the kua regarding my question about the correct order of the kua to use in my new version of the *I Ching*, I realized that the answer was not going to be in words, but that I would be shown the exact order to use. My state of excitement rose so high that I was tingling.

KING WEN'S ORDER

FU HSI'S ORDER

FU HSI'S
FIRST KUA

FU HSI'S
SECOND KUA

In Fu Hsi's order, the first kua is composed of all solid lines, and the second kua is made up of all solid lines except for the bottom line.

KING WEN'S
FIRST KUA

KING WEN'S
SECOND KUA

In King Wen's order, the first kua is also composed of all solid lines, but the second kua is composed of all broken lines. Therefore, because the first line was 3-3-3, a 9, resulting in a solid line that would change to a broken line, it could be either of the two orders since in both orders the first line of the first kua is solid and the first line of the second kua is broken.

I continued with the manipulation of the yarrow stalks, and you can imagine my excitement and anticipation as I watched the unfolding of the second line. It is at times like those when we are in full communication with All-That-Is that the wonder of the Universe can be powerfully felt. The second line was again, 3-3-3, another 9.

I knew then that the correct order for my new book was King Wen's order. I thanked All-That-Is for being so generous with me, and although I knew what the answer was, I continued with the divination to be certain. I manipulated the yarrow stalks and got another 3, then another, and then another, for the third 9. I could not continue.

I was so overwhelmed with the perfection of the response of three solid lines that became three broken lines, clearly showing me that the correct order was King Wen's, and by the trust that was placed in me by such an open communication, that I felt it would be an ungenerous, mistrustful slap in the face of All-That-Is to continue. I bowed low to my Universe, to our Universe, and ended the session. The feeling of gratitude stayed with me for months.

In the past I spent considerable time wondering how King Wen had arrived at his order of the kua, but after experiencing the discovery of which order to use for the new book, I knew how he probably arrived at his order: he did what I did, he used the yarrow stalks. The order of the kua does not affect the readings.

CHAPTER EIGHT
Precedence of the Lines

The kua we obtain as an answer describes the condition or situation surrounding our question. If any of the six lines of the kua resulted from a 6 or a 9, they are to be read as part of the answer and are called *moving lines*. Lines resulting from a 7 or an 8 are not taken into consideration as part of the answer. The text of the moving line or lines take precedence over the kua. An example will clarify this. The situation described in Kua 41, Sun, is that of decrease, but line 5 of that kua says that in the time of decrease you will be greatly increased. Because the text of the moving line takes precedence over the kua, if you obtain Line 5 as a result of a 6, you will be greatly increased even though the kua as a whole describes a time of decrease.

Lines resulting from a 6 or a 9 are called *moving lines* because they change into their opposite and form another kua. The new kua tells us what the situation or condition will become as a result of our following the counsel in the first kua. None of the lines in the second kua are to be read as part of the answer, although they may be read to get a better understanding of the kua.

MOVEMENT OF THE LINES

Following the law of eternal change, the lines are always in motion, always moving upward. As a new line enters from the bottom, it pushes the five lines above it upward, thereby displacing the line at the top. The movement is always in time to the rhythm of the universal heartbeat, always mirroring the Universe itself. Taken together, the kua and their lines represent every conceivable condition in Heaven and on Earth with all their states of change. Is that not wonderful?

CHAPTER NINE

Phrasing Questions

You can ask "yes" or "no" questions, but there are better ways to phrase your questions. The I Ching does not contain "yes" or "no" answers. But if you ask a question that requires a "yes" or "no" answer such as, "Should I marry now?" and you receive as an answer the kua of "Strong Restraint," your answer would be clear. A more meaningful answer can be obtained if you ask, "What can I expect if I marry now?" Depending on your answer, you might then want to ask, "What can I expect if I marry later?" Intelligent, well-thought-out questions will be the most rewarding.

It is essential that you write out your questions. It will also be helpful if you write a little about the conditions surrounding your question. Here is an example of what you might write:

> The house we are renting is for sale. We would like to buy the house, but it would strain our resources to the limit. My husband has just taken a new job, and there is a small

possibility that he will be transferred, which would necessitate our reselling the house. What can we expect if we buy the house now?

By writing out the conditions surrounding your question, you will find that it is easier to formulate it. Initially, you probably would think to ask whether you should buy the house now.

Writing out the conditions surrounding your question makes it clear that you should also ask what you and your husband can expect if he is transferred, and if you do not want him to be transferred, he might ask, "What can I do to avoid being transferred?"

Using the I Ching gives you the awareness that you do not have to be pushed around willy-nilly by fate, and that by taking the appropriate action you can determine your own fate. For example, asking whether you will make a lot of money this year indicates that you are not in control. A better question is, "What can I do to increase my earnings this year?" Asking what action you should take to create a particular result is always a good question and demonstrates your awareness that you can control your affairs.

Always write the date, the time, and your location at the top of the page on which you write your question for later reference.

It will also be of great benefit to write the answer to your question on the same page as that upon which you wrote your question. Keep the pages in a binder or folder so that you can refer to them at a later time. By reviewing your questions and answers occasionally, you will see how events turned out and how the answers applied.

As the years go by, you will be able to look back and see what your concerns were at different times in your life and whether they remained the same or changed. (The *I Ching Workbook*, Power Press, is designed to fill that need.)

AN EXAMPLE

Below, I have asked a question on your behalf for three reasons: first, so you will have an example to follow; second, so you can determine what you could expect in the way of help from using the I Ching; and third, so you can see how the system works. I asked the following question as if I were you.

> February 2, 2005: 7:20 A.M., Riviera Ave. house. I have
> problems and difficulties and I need help. What can
> I expect from using the I Ching?

The resulting kua is Kua 59, Huan, "Dissolve, Disintegrate, Dissipate, Unify."

The lines are:

Top Line 6	2, 2, 3 = 7	———
Line 5	3, 3, 3 = 9	———•
Line 4	3, 2, 3 = 8	— —
Line 3	3, 3, 2 = 8	— —
Line 2	3, 2, 2 = 7	———
Bottom Line 1	2, 3, 3 = 8	— —

Because Line 5 changes, this becomes Kua 4, Mêng (Inexperience).

———
— —
— —
— —
———
— —

The text of Kua 59 and the moving line are reproduced below. The five lines that are not to be taken into consideration in the answer are not reproduced. The dot at the end of Line 5 will be explained later.

KUA 59, HUAN, DISSOLVE, DISINTEGRATE, DISSIPATE, UNIFY

This indicates that a dangerous situation exists that you can resolve by identifying the danger and acting to gently dissolve or dispel the dangerous elements. The source of the danger is disunity and a lack of harmony among those who should be unified and cooperating to achieve a common goal. Human elements or traits that can prevent harmony and unity include ego, selfish and divergent self-interests, hostility, anger, greed, hard-heartedness, and even hatred. If there is a lack of enthusiasm and dedication to a common goal, creating and maintaining unity will be difficult.

To obtain help in identifying the heart of the problem and in arriving at ways to dispel the danger, seek the guidance of the Universe in whatever way is appropriate for you, such as again inquiring of the oracle. Speaking with the people involved will help you to learn what is keeping apart those who should be working together. If you make yourself a focal point; provide a common goal around which everyone can rally; and generate enthusiasm; as well as dissolving enmity, anger, hostility, and hatred, you will defeat the dangerous elements that are blocking unity. You will succeed in dissolving even the greatest danger, provided you persevere in searching for its source and in seeking ways to dissolve it. Success is certain.

Line 5: You are strong and in a position of leadership. Despite the dangerous situation at present, in which disunity and conflict prevail, you will be inspired with a great idea that will unite your group. You will communicate it with such enthusiasm that everyone will follow your inspired leadership and thus end the conflict. Remain modest, and do not take credit. Instead, share it with others, and you will remain without blame for your actions.

The kua says that by consulting the I Ching, you will be able to penetrate to the heart of your problems and dissolve them. Line 5 says that you are a strong person and implies that you are in charge of your own destiny (a position of leadership). It states specifically that you will receive inspiring ideas from the I Ching about ways to dissolve your problems. It also offers assurance, saying, "You will succeed in dissolving even the greatest danger, provided you persevere in searching for its source and in seeking ways to dissolve it." A moving line is so called because it is charged with so much energy that it turns into its opposite, a broken line into a solid line and a solid line into a broken line, thereby bringing about the formation of a new kua. Because Line 5 is a moving line, it changes into a broken line, bringing about the formation of a new kua.

The new kua describes what the situation will become, or it supplies additional information. In this case the new kua is 4, Mêng, "Inexperience." It is reproduced here except for the individual lines, which are not taken into consideration.

KUA 4, MÊNG, INEXPERIENCE

When inexperienced persons seek guidance from experienced teachers, they meet with success because it is the teacher's joy and responsibility to teach others. It is important, though, that students have the right attitude toward their teachers. These are some basic guidelines that will help.

First, students must say that they are inexperienced and need guidance.

Second, they should be modest and show the teacher proper respect.

Third, they should never mistrustfully question the teacher more than once about the same question. However, if the answer is truly not understood, additional questions are permissible. Following these simple steps will make the teacher happy to cooperate, and thus the student will continue to learn. This then becomes an amazing time for students because they can learn the great words of wisdom and become expert in their chosen field. That is how teachers lead their students to success.

If you are the teacher and your students continue to doubt your answers or do not show you the respect you deserve, it is wise to abandon your efforts. Some people are not ready to listen to the wise words of a sage. Instead, let them go out in the world, where the Universe will give them what they need for their learning. Over time, they will be molded, shaped, and changed to the point where they will be more willing to listen. There is no saying how long this will take, for it is different with everyone.

This kua offers advice for both students and teachers. You must think about the question you asked and decide which you are. Once you have decided, follow the guidance appropriate for your role.

You are being guided to seek out more information about your quest. You can do this by asking more questions of the I Ching, by researching your subject to gain a greater understanding of it, or by seeking help from a qualified person or mentor. An inexperienced person like yourself will do well to seek guidance from experienced teachers, because that will ultimately lead to your success. It is your task to seek out a teacher, for it is not appropriate for teachers to seek you out. Perseverance in learning brings success, and thoroughness in all that is done shapes character. If you fail to find your teacher or guide, you may also fail to achieve your goal. However, your inexperience, which forces you to find out more, is actually a blessing because your pursuit of knowledge will develop your character and move you further toward your enlightenment. If you proceed in that manner, you will quickly gain understanding and expertise, and you will fly to your goal like a hungry eagle when it has sighted its prey.

As you can see, Mêng states that you are inexperienced and will seek guidance from an experienced teacher. If you doubt the information and continue to ask the same question to see whether you will obtain the same response, the answer you receive will not be intelligible. The kua promises that you will have success and that the information will not be withheld from you. It goes on to say that the success you seek will be obtained by perseverance in seeking guidance and adds that by being thorough you will form character.

The information and guidance provided by Huan and Mêng yield the clear, direct, intelligent, and enlightened answers one expects from a great teacher. Providing answers of this clarity and quality has made the I Ching treasured by billions of people over thousands of years.

part four
THE SUPERIOR
PERSON

The Superior Person

In *I Ching Wisdom,* Volume I, it is stated:

> *Every person
> must have something to follow,
> a lodestar.*

Wu Wei's comment:

Everyone needs something to bring out the best in himself and to provide direction for his development. By holding the image of the superior person in your mind as your lodestar, you will achieve not only supreme success but also great happiness.

A few qualities of the superior person:

He is humble.

He is willing to let others go ahead of him.

He is courteous.

His good manners stem from his humility and concern for others.

He is good-natured.

He is calm.

He is always inwardly acknowledging the wonder he feels for all of creation.

He is willing to give another the credit.

He speaks well of everyone, ill of no one.

He believes in himself and in others.

He does not swear.

He is physically fit.

He does not overindulge.

He knows what is enough.

He can cheerfully do without.

He is willing to look within himself to find the error.

He is true to what he believes.

He is gentle.

He is able to make decisions and to act on them.

He is reverent.

He carries on his teaching activity.

He does not criticize or find fault.

He is willing to take blame.

He does not have to prove anything.

He is content within himself.

He is dependable.

He is aware of danger.

He is certain of his right to be here.

He is certain of your right to be here.

He is aware that the Universe is unfolding as it should.

He is generally happy.

He laughs easily.

He can cry.

It is all right with him if another wins.

His happiness for another's happiness is sincere.

His sorrow for another's sorrow is sincere.

He has no hidden agendas.

He is thrifty and therefore is not in want.

He finds a use for everything.

He honors everyone and is therefore honored.

He pays attention to detail.

He is conscientious.

He values everyone, and therefore everyone values him.

He is optimistic.

He is trustworthy.

He is good at salvage.

He is patient.

He knows the value of silence.

He is peaceful.

He is generous.

He is considerate.

He is fair.

He is courageous in the face of fear.

He is clean.

He is tidy.

He does not shirk his duties.

He causes others to feel special.

He expects things to turn out well.

He is always seeking to benefit others in some way.

His presence has a calming effect.

He is not attached to things.

He sees obstruction as opportunity.

He sees opposition as a signpost deflecting him in the right direction.

He sets a good example.

He is joyous of heart.

He takes thought for the future.

He wastes nothing, and therefore he always has enough.

He has good manners.

He obtains nothing by force.

He overlooks the mistakes of others.

He has greatness of spirit.

He is clear-headed.

He does more than his share.

He meets others more than halfway.

He rests when it is time to rest; he acts when it is time to act.

He feels no bitterness.

He is forgiving.

He does not pretend.

He is not cynical.

He studies.

He reveres the ancient masters.

He is inspiring.

He nourishes nature and therefore is nourished by nature.

He leaves things better than he found them.

He does not make a show.

He practices goodness.

He is simple.

His intentions are always beneficial.

He is a wellspring of determination.

He does not boast.

He produces long-lasting effects.

He has endurance.

He is flexible in his thinking.

He does not overreach himself.

He does not overspend himself.

He does not strive foolishly.

He is consistent.

He does not go into debt.

He lives a simple life.

He nurtures his good qualities and virtues.

He is sensitive to his inner prompting.

He exists in the present.

He feels no break with time.

He is cautious.

He is kind.

He holds his goals lightly in his mind, allows no opposing thoughts to enter, and, as a result of natural law, is drawn inexorably to his goals.

He seeks enlightenment.

He sets limitations for himself within which he experiences complete freedom.

He is careful of his words, knowing that he is reflected in them.

He does not use flattery.

He depends on himself for his happiness.

He feels secure.

He knows the truth of his existence.

He does not strive for wealth, fame, popularity, or possessions.

He does not complain.

He turns back immediately having discovered that he has strayed from the path of the superior person.

He practices daily self-renewal of his character.

In *I Ching Wisdom*, Volume I, it is stated:

> *Only*
> *through daily self-renewal of character*
> *can you continue*
> *at the height of your powers.*

Wu Wei's comment:

It takes Herculean effort to reach the peak of perfection in any area of life and continuous effort to remain there. Every day some effort should be expended in refreshing yourself with the ways of the superior person. Reading the *I Ching* or other great books, talking to like-minded people, teaching others, studying the deeds of our ancient heroes, thinking about your actions of the day to see whether you are being the best you can be; all are ways to successfully continue on the path. As you grow in awareness, your power grows, and your attainments will be like the harvest after a perfect summer. There is no other activity that rewards you as richly as the daily self-renewing of your character.

Index

OTHER TITLES FROM POWER PRESS

Available from your favorite neighborhood and on-line bookstores:

The Alcoholism & Addiction Cure: A Holistic Approach to Total Recovery
Breakthrough 3-Step Program from the World-Renowned
Passages Treatment Center
By Chris Prentiss, Trade Paperback, $15.95 ISBN: 0-943015-44-8

A Tale of the I Ching: How the Book of Changes Began
An Enchanted Journey Into the Origins and Workings of the I Ching
By Wu Wei, Trade Paperback, $10.95 ISBN: 0-943015-47-2

The I Ching: The Book of Answers, New Revised Edition
The Profound and Timeless Classic of Universal Wisdom
By Wu Wei, Trade Paperback, $15.95 ISBN: 0-943015-41-3

I Ching Wisdom: Guidance from the Book of Answers, Volume I,
New Revised Edition
Practical Insights for Creating a Life of Success and Good Fortune
By Wu Wei, Trade Paperback, $12.95 ISBN: 0-943015-42-1

50 Yarrow Stalks from China
Handpicked by farmers in northeast China specifically for use with the
I Ching
50 7" yarrow stalks, $10.95 ISBN: 0-943015-05-7
50 10" yarrow stalks, $12.95 ISBN: 0-943015-45-6

Bookstores, please contact SCB Distributors toll free at 800-729-6423.
Tel: 310-532-9400. Fax: 310-532-7001. E-mail: info@scbdistributors.com.
Web site: www.scbdistributors.com.

COLLECTIBLE TITLES
AVAILABLE DIRECTLY FROM THE PUBLISHER*

I Ching Wisdom: Volume II, More Guidance from the Book of Changes
I Ching Life: Living It
The I Ching Handbook: Getting What You Want
The I Ching Workbook
The Zen of Happiness
The God Game

*To order these collectible titles from Power Press, write, call, or e-mail:
 Power Press, 6428 Meadows Court, Malibu, California, 90265.
 Tel: 310-392-9393. E-mail: wuwei@power-press.com.
 Web site: www.power-press.com.